African Cinema and Urbanism

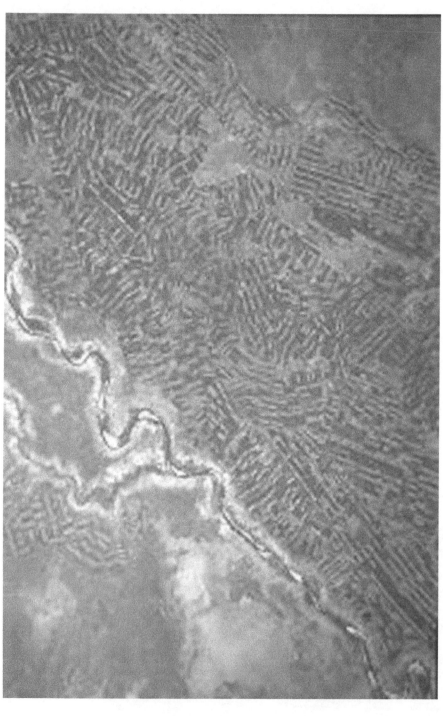

Figure 0.1 Sudan Agriculture along Blue Nile, near Khartoum. Attribution: Courtesy NASA/Lunar and Planetary Institute.

African Cinema and Urbanism

Marie-Paule Macdonald

ANTHEM PRESS

Anthem Press
An imprint of Wimbledon Publishing Company
www.anthempress.com

This edition first published in UK and USA 2024
by ANTHEM PRESS

75–76 Blackfriars Road, London SE1 8HA, UK
or PO Box 9779, London SW19 7ZG, UK
and
244 Madison Ave #116, New York, NY 10016, USA

British Library Cataloguing-in-Publication Data
A catalogue record for this book is available from the British Library.

Library of Congress Cataloging-in-Publication Data: 2024941646
A catalog record for this book has been requested.

ISBN-13: 978-1-83999-107-3 (Pbk)
ISBN-10: 1-83999-107-0 (Pbk)

Cover Credit: Renée Dotson, of the Library and Publication Services,
USRA/Lunar and Planetary Institute

This title is also available as an e-book.

Dedication to Wangarĩ Maathai, 2004
Nobel Peace Prize laureate

CONTENTS

FIGURES

ACKNOWLEDGEMENTS

I gratefully acknowledge the impact of the films, their directors and crews, as well as the key influence of film festivals, their researchers and the lasting records kept by analysts, writers and critics, in particular African film festivals such as Vues d'Afrique in Montreal and FESPACO in Ougadougou.

I would like to recognize the invaluable editing contributed by Nichola Lewis.

For a fundamental grounding in urban theory, urbanism and heritage, I extend my sincere appreciation to Françoise Choay.

INTRODUCTION

In a 20-minute interview, Djibril Diop Mambéty (1945–1998) was asked how to make a movie, to which he responded with a monologue:

> You want to know how to make movies, is that it? OK, to make movie, it's simple. One closes the eyes. Have you closed your eyes? You close your eyes. You see points of light. Shut your eyes tightly. The points become clearer. People come into focus. Life is created. The mind works, but not more than the heart. A whole story unfolds in the direction of the wind that you want. The story is here, and then you open your eyes and have a story. Do the same thing. Voilà.[1]

In this micro-performance, the film director Mambéty, who filmed the locations where he lived, places that he knew and frequented in Dakar, reveals an inner landscape of cinematic creation from the beginning, familiar and yet *ex novo*. This study of documentary and dramatic African film is viewed through cinematic portals and is intended to interpret the post-colonial environment and to anticipate the future; a range of examples of African film and video – documentary and fiction – present, evaluate and critique the transformation of urban and rural landscapes in Africa. Operating from differing points of view and at varying levels of investigation, these chapters demonstrate the development and professionalization of African cinema over the years, and also discuss the role cinema plays in highlighting these landscapes by juxtaposing the empirical data that the moving image provides, and in relation to the various domains within, that may not be similar but may adjoin and interconnect. The visual and aural nature of cinema and its photographic and documentary character also allow for the discussion and critique of contemporary issues in the urban and rural dynamic of development, from related subjects on climate change, such as deforestation, sustainability and biodiversity, water and food supply, inequity and women's rights, political instability, security and sovereignty.

These selected works comprise multiplatform digital video, cinema and streamed moving images, which, with an emphasis on documentaries, open the door to rethinking and eventually to the possibilities of fresh proposals responding to the situations portrayed. Cinematic media convey important visual information regarding the urban and rural built environments in Africa's numerous geographic zones and diverse territories that are projected for major evolution and development over the coming decades. By 2050, rapid unplanned urban development is likely to have characterized Africa's landscape, along with many other forms of urbanization, which are vividly described in works by the social theorist AbdouMaliq Simone. Former colonial metropoles and urban centres, with their historic cores and symbolic landmarks, still retain a certain cultural heft that can offer possibilities for establishing new affiliations. These African cities are navigable and negotiable areas acting as clearing houses and crucibles, where there may be more possibilities to forge distinct, diverse identities than in rural areas, villages and towns.

During the pandemic, when travel was curtailed, small screens became significant, even the primary interfaces for human communication, which widened and emphasized the digital divide. Ever more influential, the small screens of mobile phones came to convey important visual and aural information regarding the major changes and developments projected over the next 30 years for urban and rural built environments in Africa's numerous geographic zones. Definitions and practices in the use of public and private space during the pandemic were adopted for significant periods of time. The way in which citizens accessed public infrastructure such as clinics and temporary modifications to streets and parks, for example, imparted a sense of elasticity of usage. The lessening perception of centrality and centralized urban locations led to relocation, individualized workplaces and an atomized workforce. Offices located in dense city centres that formerly relied on centralized, specialized expertise now had to function with digital input by dispersed creators, which resulted in a confluence of combined components rendering the screen as a primary interface for multiple disciplines.

Even though screens were small and singular and, often as not, watched by a lone viewer, there was more collective access than ever to streamed information and screen media. While viewing onscreen was an isolated experience, whether for work, leisure or relationships, much activity, even conferences and film festivals, converged for exchanges via remote communication software. In parallel, creative work in architecture and urbanism, design work that traditionally was a component of team and collective brainstorming, also became a more individualized creative process, as co-workers no longer shared the same workspace.

The adjustment period between pandemic and endemic and the abundance of online information have led to other possibilities in architecture and urbanism and a reluctance to return to the pre-pandemic status quo in the approach to urban space. The elasticities of public space usage may influence changes in the built environment as societies reconsider urban development in the aftermath of the pandemic, as well as addressing climate change. There may be a lag between considering the kinds of built environment that citizens may want and obtaining effective public input, feedback and participation in the decision-making process, which is often controlled by property owners and developers. In terms of building types, contemporary urbanism questions the utility of modern, high-rise or tall glass buildings, whether underway or recently completed, if not the very concept of centralized, downtown business districts. Although tall towers are fundamentally more harmful environmentally and vulnerable to climate change, largely due to their energy inefficiencies and factors such as their elevator dependence, they may be aggressively advertised and marketed until owners gauge whether they will ever be fully occupied or will be sold off due to weak demand – given the so-called stickiness of real estate prices.

One purpose of this book is to further speculate on the after-effects of the pandemic on urban and territorial form and the development of the built environment. There are now strong preferences for remote work and an ongoing critique of empty downtown office towers, which are inefficient and unpopular. Similarly, critiques of accepted norms in relation to urban and rural landscapes, foodscape and food autonomy and security, and supply chains and transport have emerged as a reaction to pandemic and race issues, and have led to questions about what this portends for interconnecting developing areas of the world, such as the African continent. These are questions to be addressed holistically, particularly when considering African urban and rural landscapes under pressure from many forces – migration, population growth, climate change, health and food security.

Author and educator Lesley Lokko, founder of the African Futures Institute in Accra, Ghana, states that 'what you know is largely dependent on where you are' and that one's world view is shaped thus, as is 'one's place within it' (at 8 minutes). She advocates that one 'live through imagination' (at 46 minutes).[2] During the pandemic, many conferences and meetings showcased African participants, experts, theorists, designers, architects and urbanists, who, in the impetus of a planetary-scaled new normal, reached into home workplaces in African cities. These kinds of interventions provide a foundation for this current research.

Paying close attention to a range of media can provide a listening and observation forum. The visual and sound information furnished by screen imagery is material in motion that can be absorbed and analysed, and could lead to concretizing ideas, conventions and possibilities for urban landscapes in Africa.

Another goal of this book is to contribute to critical discourse and knowledge resources, to assess, critique and propose directions in contemporary urban and settlement development in the face of rapid spontaneous urbanization of landscapes in a context of climate change and housing need and to study, track and present options for landscapes and cities in Africa that are intrinsic to African culture via documentary and narrative cinema, incorporating diverse platforms.

This work brings together theories and practices from the disciplines of urbanism, architecture and African cinema studies to examine some examples of how African filmmakers and, by extension, urbanists, architects, designers, thinkers and artists are bringing attention to issues of urban precarity, climate change, survival and growth, and creativity on the continent. Theories such as Felwine Sarr's theory of 'Afrotopias' or 'Afrotopos' posit that the continent is a formidable site for creative potential:

> Afrotopos is this a site of another Africa, one whose arrival we should expedite in order to realize its brilliant potentials. Founding a utopia is not at all a question of simply giving oneself over to sugar-coated reveries, but a matter of thinking spaces of the real to bring them into existence by way of both thought and action; it's about recognizing the signs and seeds of the present day in order to better nourish them. Afrotopia is an active utopia that takes as its task the cultivation of vast and open spaces of bountiful possibles in order to help them flourish.[3]

Another theoretical influence with a significant impact on contemporary African cities is the term 'Black urbanism' as proposed by AbdouMaliq Simone. An alternative to modernist western urbanism, the concept recognizes the ad hoc nature of urban development in its informality, creativity and improvization. Simone explains his theory as bringing together 'different strands of critical Black thought' to engage with urban life and activities. He classifies this process as speculative thought on the topic, viewing the urban as not necessarily coherent but nevertheless 'tangible, material and not abstract' so as to 'extend the understanding of urban', given the 'fundamental incompleteness of urbanization' with reference to the French urban philosopher and sociologist Henri Lefebvre.[4] Other readers of Simone qualify his approach as a shift in order to perceive new global assemblages of human ecology in urban environments, with a suggested reference to Deleuzean philosophy.[5]

Chapter 1 considers cinematic visions of settlements in their territories and villages and cities in their landscapes. Film presents specificities of place, society, environment and culture in its time, and these early works in African cinema emphasize an oral culture. Ousmane Sembène's *Borom Sarret* (1963), with its lucid social critique, is set in the modern and traditional districts of post-independence Dakar and depicts a day in the life of a wagoner who thinks about his surroundings out loud, in voiceover, as he goes about his business. Also discussed is Sembène's *Ceddo*, or *Outsiders* (1977), a key work of complex oratory in a historical setting. *Ceddo* unveils a future convergence of neo-colonialist regimes and imperialism. Safi Faye's docufiction *Lettre paysanne* (1975), to some extent juxtaposes an incompatible ethos of urban versus village life while subtly intertwining a spoken narrative with documentary film convention. *Yeelen* (1987) by Souleymane Cissé stands out for its mythical portrayal of Dogon landscapes and magical powers materializing out of the landscape, biomes and vast territories. The fiction film *Zan Boko* (1988), by Gaston Kaboré, layers the process of the erosion of traditional compound housing and village life in Burkina Faso as Ouagadougou extends its reach into the countryside. In this context, there has been much media debate within technological media culture in the context of Ouagadougou, and its relevance is further commented on, after a streamed screening of Kaboré's *Zan Boko* in 2014 by architect Jean-Philippe Vassal, who worked as an urbanist in Niamey in the 1980s, and who mentions his perception of these themes in the context of emerging urban planning of the era.

Chapter 2 addresses demographic shifts, population growth, dispersion and migration scenarios in the context of ever-increasing reliance on long-lasting, extensive refugee camps. Urbanists speculate that the many various types of refugee camps may influence the forms of settlement under the pressures of impending intense rural urbanization. The films discussed include the highly effective radical and autobiographical approach of Med Hondo's narrative docufiction in *Soleil Ô* (1970), which explores the sometimes disingenuous reactions by the French to the mid-twentieth century swell of African immigration to their country. The now influential 1973 drama *Touki-Bouki* (*The Journey of the Hyena*) by Djibril Diop Mambéty, takes a ludic and original stance on migration; and his later film drama *Hyenas* (1992), presents yet another satirical posture on society and village life. The last film directed by Djibril Diop Mambéty (released posthumously, 1998), *La Petite Vendeuse de Soleil* (*The Little Girl Who Sold the Sun*), is also briefly discussed for its engagement with Dakar districts and street life. It is a short drama film with a lively, youthful narrative about an irrepressible young woman that reflects on children and disability in Dakar. In this context, the director's work has been commented upon by the critic and academic Françoise Pfaff, much of whose work explores the urban specificity of the locales and city settings in the work of a range of influential directors, including Mambéty and Sembène. Thomas Loubière's *Le Camp suspendu* (2020) observes the lengthy stays and frustrating stasis of refugees, or returnees (retournés), those returning from the Central

African Republic who live in camps in Chad and appear to be in limbo. The film by Ousmane Zoromé Samassékou, *Le dernier refuge* (*The Last Shelter,* 2021*)*, set in Gao, Mali, gives voice to the youth who leave their homelands. And *The Writer from a Country without Bookstores* (2019), a film directed by Marc Serena, follows writer Juan Tomás Ávila Laurel from Equatorial Guinea – self-exiled in Barcelona since 2011 – on a return visit; during which he chafes at the limits of a static society under the long-enduring dictatorship and telepresence of the country's president, Teodoro Obiang Nguema Mbasogo, and he meets with playwrights and writers who must carry their publications with them. Hind Meddeb and Thim Naccache's *Paris Stalingrad* (2019) documents the urban encampments of refugees in Paris's nineteenth arrondissement and the local authorities' controversial actions in response to the phenomenon.

Chapter 3 focusses on urbanization, infrastructure and landscape; the phenomenon of modern landscapes of extraction, megaprojects, megacities and new cities, as well as the landscapes of informal cities such as Kibera in Nairobi, Kenya, where work is being carried out by the Kounkuey Design Initiative (KDI). The chapter explores a range of modes of urbanization as represented in contemporary African films, which include streamed video explanations of the Kibera projects. The documentary *Arlit, Deuxième Paris (Arlit, the Second Paris,* 2004), directed by Idrissou Mora-Kpaï, reports on the decline of a city and mining region in Niger and its related ecological fallout. *Anbessa* (2019) by Mo Scarpelli highlights the issues of unequal distribution of housing in Ethiopia's Addis Ababa at a time of rapid urbanization when arrays of new multi-storey housing blocks sprang up in its suburban peripheries and displaced land dwellers, who were left to squat in makeshift dwellings. The documentary *143 rue du désert (143 Sahara Street,* 2019), directed by Hassen Ferhani, is set in the Algerian desert and follows the story of a mostly transitory community that frequents a traditional rest stop run by a lone older woman, whose business is threatened by the construction of a large, modern service station and the eventual transformation and modernization of a vast slice of desert territory.

Chapter 4 addresses hybridity: Chinese, European, Soviet, North and South American influences; cultural critiques and theoretical influences; infrastructural influences; and the recent influence of urban intervention by China, transitioning from the prior influence of the Soviet era. The far-reaching impact of Chinese investment on African infrastructure and, by extension, on its social daily spaces has made China the continent's largest trading and debt partner. The economic effects of the pandemic slowed the pace of Chinese investment activity. The films analysed and discussed in this chapter include the Rwandan director Yuhi Amuli's *A Taste of Our Land* (2020); a Sudanese short film *Al-Sit* (2020) by Suzannah Mirghani; *Days of Cannibalism:*

of Pioneers, Cows and Capital (2020) by Teboho Edkins; and Nicole Schafer's *Buddha in Africa* (2020), which critiques the so-called soft power, or cultural interventions, of Chinese-run orphanages in Malawi.

Chapter 5 deals with the futurities and technologies of the moving image, socio-cultural movements and cultural restitution. The science-fiction short film *Pumzi* (2009), by the Nairobi-based director Wanuri Kahiu, imagines a dystopian future world and explores the layered contemporary meanings of Afrofuturism. Kahiu's feature fiction film, *Rafiki* (2018), addresses gay rights while offering glimpses of contemporary housing in Nairobi. Controversial issues of cultural restitution are addressed in the 2020 documentary *Restituer l'art africain, les fantômes de la colonisation.* (Returning Art to Africa, the Ghosts of Colonisation, 2021) by Laurent Védrine. The impact of mid-century modern architecture, and its re-evaluation as large-scale sculpture, is the subject of the film *Maison Tropicale* (2008) by Manthia Diawara. Its departure point discusses the removed work of mid-twentieth-century French architect and designer Jean Prouvé. The documentary outlines the trajectory of portable housing prototypes destined for tropical climates, erected in Niamey and Brazzaville, whose value soared when reassessed in Europe as design objects. The chapter ends with a discussion of contemporary projects by several influential architects whose work is disseminated via streamed digital video. These examples anticipate the impact of urbanization predicted to take place over many regions of the African continent.

Chapter 6 addresses immediate questions of sustainability, biomes, biodiversity, and reforestation and sustainability strategies. Contemporary film has occupied the forefront, playing a major role in public education and advocacy concerning environmental justice. This selection covers a range of issues, demonstrating the complex interaction of environmental themes, economic development, women's issues, traditional social structures and often featuring the prime question of water scarcity. Filmed between 2018 and 2020, Aïssa Maïga's *Marcher sur l'eau* (*Above Water*, 2021) follows the seasons in the lives of formerly nomadic Fulani settlements and demonstrates an effective solution to the water shortage, namely deep well drilling. The cinematography depicts a magnificent landscape and way of life, which plagued by drought, will be impacted by the proposed regional drilling of deep boreholes for wells and eventually lead to reintroducing pastures and vegetation in Niger. The docufiction feature *Aya* (2021) directed by Simon Coulibaly Gillard highlights the effects of coastal erosion. Addressing forestry on a global scale is Luc Marescot's *Poumon Vert et Tapis Rouge* (Green Forests and the Red Carpet, 2021), inspired by the botanist Francis Hallé's tropical forest research. Malam Saguirou's documentary film *Solaire Made in Africa* (2017), demonstrates the continuing relevance of the direct solar technologies advocated decades ago by Professor Abdou Moumouni Dioffo in Niger. Lastly, several short films that address ecological themes include Anjali Nayar's *Oil and Water* (2020). This 15-minute short concisely condenses the conflict affecting Turkana women in settlements in northern Kenya and their traditional responsibilities of providing daily water and their access to it in the face of the community's negotiation with a British oil company that reneged on its commitments. The short documentary *Lucie* (2019), directed by Marlyse Awa Yotomane, depicts the nature of daily work for a rural woman in the Central African Republic. The role of Malian rural women carrying out the ancestral maintenance of earthen homes in Siby is documented in *Bogo Ja*, (2020). Directed by Soussaba Cissé, it further develops themes on women's roles in shaping the built environment. Seidou Samba Touré's documentary, *Massiiba, le mal d'un people*, (Massiiba, The Misfortunes of a People, 2020), documents the effects of unrest and political instability in Burkina Faso. It is a credit to the director's courage and energy to disseminate this investigative reporting of what is called an invisible war.

In reviewing the goals of this research, it is worth keeping in mind the perspective of Okwui Enwezor, a Nigerian and the first non-European artistic director of *Documenta*, in the Documenta 11 exhibition publication, *Platform 4 Under Siege: Four African Cities, Freetown, Johannesburg, Kinshasa, Lagos (2002)*, in which he frames an overview of urban issues:

> As any other urban space around the world, African cities are of course centres for the migration and refuge of increasing numbers of people. As such they are also the meeting place and battleground for two conflicting worlds of power and impotence, wealth and poverty, corruption and hope, centre and periphery. But the issue we want to emphasize is that African cities are not only outlined by these troubling bifurcations. Nor do we wish to reproduce only the image of cities riddled with crime, grinding poverty, overcrowded suburbs, and shanty towns, congested living spaces which usually lack essential services and are breeding grounds of disease, ethnic violence, high mortality rate, or the persistent degradation of their environments. These are certainly important issues which need addressing. Yet, our attention is persistently called to focus on the ethical accounting of these cities' dynamism as hosts of great potentials which challenge the often gloomy, doomsday pictures painted by the popular media.[6]

Notes

1 Matthias Turcaud, review, 'La petite vendeuse de soleil, les "petites gens dans la lumière"', *Africa Vivre* (website) including an interview with Djibril Diop Mambéty (accessed 15 December 2023) https://www.africavivre.com/senegal/a-voir/films /la-petite-vendeuse-de-soleil-les-petites-gens-dans-la-lumiere.html. Djibril Diop

Mambéty, 'Vous posez la question de savoir, Comment on fait le cinema, c'est ça? Alors, pour faire du cinema, c'est simple. Il faut fermer les yeux. Est-ce que vous avez fermé les yeux? Alors vous fermez les yeux. Vous voyez des points de lumière. Serrez fort. Les lumières se précisent. Il y a des personnages, la vie se crée, la tête fonctionne, mais pas plus que le coeur. Il y a toute une histoire qui se créer selon la direction du vent que vous voulez. L'histoire se crée. Voilà. Et puis on ouvre les yeux, on a une histoire. Faites la même chose. C'est très simple ..A chaque fois que vous voulez voir la lumière, il faut fermer les yeux'. (at 2 minutes)

2 Lesley Lokko, 'All Must Fall', lecture at the Architectural Association, London, 12 February 2019 (accessed 23 May 2022) https://www.youtube.com/watch?v =KLPSz3ItW78.

3 Felwine Sarr, *Afrotopia*. Trans. Drew S. Burke and Sarah Jones-Boardman. Minneapolis: University of Minessota Press, 2020, p. xiv. From the original publication by: [L'Afrotopos est ce lieu autre de l'Afrique don't il faut hâter la venue, car réalisant ses potentialities heureuses. Fonder une utopie, ce n'est point se laisser aller à une douce reverie, mais penser des espaces du réel à faire advenir par la pensée et l'action; c'est en réparer les signes et les germes dans le temps présent, afin de les nourrir.] Felwine Sarr, *Afrotopia*. Paris: Philippe Rey, 2016.

4 AbdouMaliq Simone, 'Black urbanism', lecture at the School of Materialist Research, 18 August 2022, at 5 min., 10–11 min., and 12 min (accessed 23 September 2022) https://www.youtube.com/watch?v=ReZOZuZv0Ns.

5 Charles Lemert, Series Editor, foreword to *City Life from Jakarta to Dakar: Movement on the Crossroads*, by AbdouMaliq Simone. New York and London: Routledge, 2010, p. xi

6 Okwui Enwezor, introduction to *Platform 4 Under Siege: Four African Cities, Freetown, Johannesburg, Kinshasa, Lagos*. Stuttgart: Hatje Cantz; New York, 2002 (accessed 15 May 2024) https://www.documenta-platform6.de/wpcontent/uploads/enwezor _platform_4_under-siege_four-african-cities.pdf and https://www.documenta.de/en /retrospective/documenta11#.

Chapter 1

INDEPENDENT VISIONS: SETTLEMENTS, TERRITORIES, LANDSCAPE, VILLAGE AND CITY

The transformations of African landscapes, from rural to urbanized spaces, have engaged African media producers since the emergence of the African film industry in the 1960s. This chapter selects key early films in African cinema by filmmakers recognized as groundbreaking innovators who contributed to the canon of early African cinema, as it developed along with independence movements. Many early productions address the urban and post-colonial contexts, when compared to later films on the rural and pre-colonial settlements and ways of life that aim to educate audiences to value and safeguard traditional African cultural values, and advocate traditional and often rural ideals. The directors were pathfinders in terms of their social vision, working somewhat in parallel, if not necessarily in accord, with the French New Wave and *auteur* theory.

Ousmane Sembène, *Borom Sarret* (*The Wagoner, Le Charretier*), Senegal, 1963, 20 Minutes

Borom Sarret visualizes a day in the life of a cart driver who risks entering the modernized, official districts of post-independence Dakar, where horse carts are forbidden and their drivers do not usually stray beyond the Indigenous, informal districts. The film represents the city as a site of possibility for some, while those like the wagoner continue to be marginalized on the outskirts of what is effectively a segregated zone of Dakar's Plateau – its exclusionary spaces functioning as obstacles in daily living. (See Figure 1.1.)

In the director's first acclaimed short film, Dakar's social layers unravel into restricted zones. The title, *Borom Sarret*, possibly derives from the French expression *bonhomme charretier* (the good wagoner). In under 20 minutes, the film compresses the principles of a socio-political critique that the body of Sembène's work aspired to: attention to fundamental post-colonial issues,

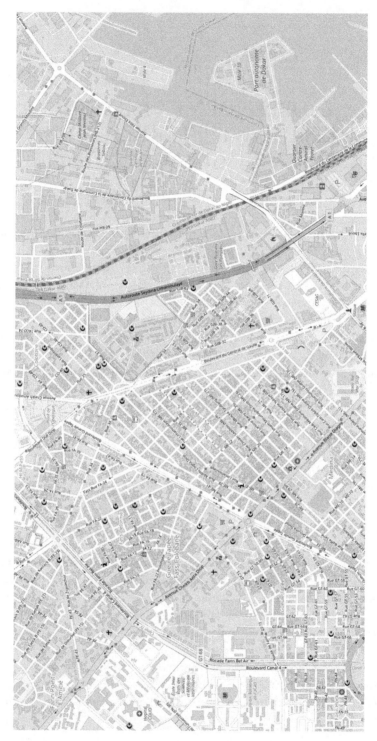

Figure 1.1 Senegal, Dakar, Colobane and Port, courtesy Open Street Map. (Film referenced: *Borom Saret*.)

critique of class exploitation, corruption, Eurocentric modernism, and attention to workers' and women's issues are presented in a socialist realist mode made riveting by an unrelenting criticism that spares no one. As summarized by Amadou T. Fofana, the unequivocal narrative 'contains all the thematic seeds' of Sembène's oeuvre.[1]

The film opens with views of the mosque and a prayer scene, and then the camera lens travels over the sandy roads and streets of an improvised settlement, as the wagon driver sets off to encounter those who need a ride but are not included in the cash economy and have no means to pay him.

The camera pans over the roofscapes as the cart driver muses and voices an inner monologue while traversing the city and listening as a wheel develops a squeak. En route to the market, he picks up a few regulars, and then a couple – the woman is heavily pregnant and leans on his shoulder until they arrive at the Maternité Mandel hospital. Later, he takes a man carrying his child's body to the cemetery, where entry is refused for lack of papers. At noon, he eats pieces of kola nut that his wife gave him, and while on a break, he ends up handing over his earnings to a charming Griot who sings his ancestors' praises.

A well-dressed young man persuades the wagoner to carry his belongings to the Plateau. Against a panoramic view of modern Dakar in the distance (at 12 minutes), the music segues into baroque chamber music in counterpoint to the squeaky wheel, and then an aerial view of the cart shows the driver risking entry to the modern downtown, transgressing the urban spatial hierarchy. In a stroke of bad luck, he is confronted by a uniformed officer. Fumbling for his papers, he drops his war medallion and ends up losing it, when the officer clamps his boot over it, confiscates the cart and sends the driver off, walking with his horse and the prospect of a fine to pay.

As he nears his home, he consoles himself and reflects, musing, 'Ça c'est la vie moderne, ici c'est mon quartier, je me sens bien'. ('That's modern life [...] this is my neighbourhood, I feel good here'). He must still face his wife and admit that his day has not gone at all well, and she then rushes off to find a way to provide dinner for the family.

Ousmane Sembène, *Ceddo*, (*Outsiders*) Senegal, 1977, 120 Minutes

Ceddo (Outsiders) remains a deftly told, portentous morality tale or parable set in an evocative landscape that introduces the imminent intersection of neo-colonialist regimes and imperialism. This poetic film remains a key work in what is known as revolutionary Third Cinema, cinematic work that aspires to rethink the present. Its title is taken from the name given to the last holders of African animist spiritualism before any Islamic or Christian influence. It is set in an imagined seventeenth century and condenses the spiritual conversion of common people, a lengthy process, into the interval of the narrative, with added dreamlike flash-forward scenes.

The film opens with a series of brief setup scenes showing the refined beauty of the landscape and traditional vernacular structures: a woman bathing in a river, then two women using poles to lift the woven grass roof off a granary, and the narrative launches in the main compound's open space, accompanied by Manu Dibangu's distinctively animated soundtrack.

In an act of resistance to forced collective conversion from animist spirituality to the monotheistic religion Islam, a Ceddo warrior (Mamadou N'Diaye Diagne) abducts Princess Dior Yacine (Tabata Ndiaye) and holds her captive, but unbound, in a nearby temporary camp and places a symbolic rope threshold on the ground. Her father, King Demba Wâr Thioub (Makhourédia Guèye), and his court must take decisive action in a time when traditions are in flux. Lengthy discourses must be exchanged in the compound's collective public space and repeated through the king's mediator, Jarâf (Oumar Gueye). The king summons all, the royal court and all his subjects, who appear before him in a ritual gathering accompanied by drumbeats. Positioned at a middle distance, the camera captures the pageantry of the rituals of the royal Wolof Court's solemn ceremonial proceedings that Michael Atkinson likened to those of Greek tragedy.[2]

The pretenders to hierarchical succession each plead a case to determine who will liberate the princess. Saxewar (Nar Sene) is her betrothed; Madior Fatim Fall (Moustapha Yade), Demba Wâr's sister's son, is heir according to traditional custom. Prince Birima (Mamadou Dioum), the king's son and according to the Islamic law, new to the kingdom, is the king's heir. The Imam (Alioune Fall) clarifies the position to the sound of snapping fingers of the raised hands of his followers surrounding him. Each contender pronounces a discourse. Madior is refused – he counters that the king is in power due to the people and he renounces his religion. Birima is chosen, and the king's subjects disperse to ritual drumming. In the following scene, the king orders bundles of sticks to be carried away and piled up for a bonfire, to provide light. Then the scene jump cuts, and gospel music plays over the scene of a group of shackled slaves being fed and also being painfully branded with a hot iron that leaves the scar of a fleur-de-lis.

Biram is killed in action trying to rescue the princess. The camera then follows Saxewar as he prepares for combat. When he arrives at the Ceddo's encampment, he is fooled into believing he has shot the kidnapper. Saxewar repositions the symbolic rope confining Princess Dior Yacine, but although he is armed with two rifles, the Ceddo blinds, disarms and then kills him.

Holding an arrow at close range, the Ceddo thrusts it into his throat. The princess looks on, impassive.

When the king dies in the night – allegedly from a snake-bite – the Imam usurps power, and there is talk of marrying the princess to him. The Imam's disciples on horseback kill the Ceddo as he lifts his arms high to load his bow and arrow – he is buried in a mound in the same position as he is killed.

As she is returned to the village, the camera moves to a spectacular close-up of the princess, who, as Sembène described her, is 'the incarnation of modern Africa'.[3] She grasps a rifle and steps forward, and Manu Dibango's lyrical, ambulatory thematic music hits a high note at the climax of the narrative. It is hardly surprising that Sembène's critique of monotheistic religious movements caused the film to be censored by the Senghor regime. It remained so until 1983 by Senegalese authorities.[4]

Safi Faye, *Lettre paysanne* (*Kaddu Beykat, Letter from My Village*), Senegal, 1975, 90 Minutes

This work of docufiction, a cinematic version of autofiction, opposes the ethos of the city and extols village life as it builds an attack on capitalism, industrialized society and colonization. The film outlines how the introduction of peanut monoculture by the French during colonial expansion has depleted the land. The pacing embraces the slower seasonal time of the village alongside the hurried, oppressive, callous and exploitative tempo in the city of Dakar.

Kaddu Beykat (*Letter from My Village*, 1975) is the first feature film to be directed by a sub-Saharan African woman. Its title can be translated as the 'words of the farmers', and the film's location is closely connected to Faye's own rural community 100 kilometres south of Dakar, near the coast in Fad'jal, a Serer village where she grew up. The region is part of Senegal's agricultural peanut basin, with about half of the country's rural population involved in peanut farming, and which continues to face issues of barren soil and minimal productivity. Contemporary discourse centres on ecological restoration of arable land. Peanut monoculture was introduced under the French colonial regime as part of an industrialized supply chain linked to Marseilles peanut oil factories.[5] Faye's film expresses a perspective that reflects her ethnographic training, while remaining attached to her terroir, her rural ancestry and traditional agrarian culture.

Kaddu Beykat looks at the impact of low-yield crops on individual aspirations. In the storyline, Ngor (Assane Faye) and Coumba (Maguelle Gueye) plan to marry and have waited two years for the harvests to improve so they can start a family. Ngor is obliged to leave and search for work in the unfamiliar streets of Dakar, where he encounters urban class systems: an urban bourgeois and petit bourgeois class structure, unknown in rural villages. Dakar's urban citizens are exploitative, and Ngor soon realizes that the work he is required to undertake for wages in the city is the lowest-ranked of all daily activities.

A contemporary short film by German director Mabel Gundlach, entitled *Saving Senegal's Peanut Basin* (2015), comprises interviews with Senegalese farmers and spokespersons for several farming collectives and organizations, who advocate ethical farming and criticize the monoculture practices of industrial farming. The organic farmer Ibrahima Seck discusses how he and others succeeded in organizing a local co-operative and producing peanut oil locally. He emphasizes the importance of a global shift to 'biological and agro-ecological' approaches to restore fertility and soil productivity.[6]

Souleymane Cissé, *Yeelen,* (La lumière, The Light), Mali, 1987, 105 Minutes

This film has been interpreted as a parable about corruption of power and generational conflict set in an inventively imagined Malian Empire in the thirteenth century. Land, magical power and spirituality are paramount in the protagonist's initiation journey through Dogon, Fulani (or Peul in French) and Bambara territories in this allegory for contemporary society.

Soma Diarra (Niamanto Sanogo) belongs to the Malian Empire's secret traditional sorcerer and blacksmith society and is enraged at the possibility that the magical powers of his son Nianankoro (Issiaka Kane) would eventually overwhelm his own. Accompanied by two servant men carrying the Kolonnkalani, a large, magic pestle that tracks its prey, he seeks out his son's location and sets off on a quest to destroy him. Using their own divining powers, Nianankoro and his mother, Mah (Soumba Traore), peer into a cauldron and watch a watery image of Soma tracking him. Mah counsels her son to flee. He heads 500 miles (880 km) south towards the Bandiagara escarpment and its Dogon villages to find his father's blind twin, Djigui Diarra.

On the way, he has many adventures that include being captured by the Fulani and taken to their King Rouma Boll (Balla Moussa Keita). While in captivity, he demonstrates his magician's prowess, performing spells that deploy swarms of bees or the powers of a termite hill. He also learns from the king's wise and empathetic governance.

In scenes where she pours millet milk over her body while standing in the river, Mah invokes the river goddess to further protect her son.[7] Nianankoro marries Attou (Aoua Sangara), another powerful female character, and when they reach Dogon country, they bathe in the sacred Bongo spring. Attou is pregnant, and Djigui Diarra divines that she will bear a son, which leads to a potent, symbolic ending sequence with poetic abstract visuals of blinding desert light.

The cinema historian Suzanne H. McRae has written about the underlying themes of light as a means of creation and destruction in the 'cosmology, anthropology, and ethics of the Komo divine knowledge' portrayed in *Yeelen*. McRae specifies that 'the major male characters in the film belong to the powerful secret Komo society, an ancient association of blacksmith/ sorcerers which forms the central Mande social institution'. And then she quotes one of their incantations: 'Heat makes fire and the two worlds – earth and sky – exist through light'.[8]

Gaston Kaboré, *Zan Boko* (*Homeland*), Burkina Faso, 1988, 95 Minutes

Gaston Kaboré is perhaps better known for his award-winning films, *Wend Kuuni* and its sequel, *Buud Yam*, that are set within historical situations and narratives of the early nineteenth century. *Buud Yam* follows the adventures of the young man Wend Kuuni, who, travelling on horseback, traverses a wide range of evocative towns and villages, with scenes of desert markets and earthen brick settlements evoking a pre-colonial way of life. (See Figure 1.2.)

At the end of the 1980s, the city of Ouagadougou had a rapidly growing population of some 500,000 and was developing at an intense pace, with about 60 per cent of unregistered urban property.[9] The municipality's inevitable expansion impinged on Indigenous land and tradition, and transformed rural compounds and villages into numbered properties to be exchanged in a market economy. A new class of affluent Ouagadougou city dwellers purchased property lots upon which they built luxurious modern villas and ushered in an era of new ways of living, which replaced governance traditions and erased traditional compound housing and its values, social relationships and collective destinies.

Kaboré's drama *Zan Boko* is the story of the village of Seloghin, situated on what was then the city edge of Ouagadougou, capital of Burkina Faso. The urbanizing process begins by annexing and numbering the traditional village houses and launching new modes of modern bureaucratic urban planning that absorb and efface rural dwelling patterns and an agrarian way of life. A scene in the film shows a boy, in an act of resistance, rubbing away a freshly painted number on an earthen enclosure wall, put there by a team of municipal employees.

The film's title, *Zan Boko*, means 'where the placenta is buried' – underscoring the profound ties to the ancestral terroir and opens with scenes of the traditional Mossi way of life and its traditions. Tinga Yerbanga (Joseph

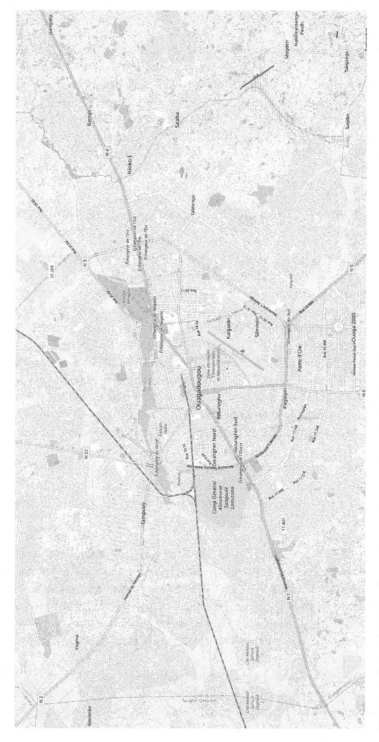

Figure 1.2 Burkina Faso, Ouagadougou, courtesy Open Street Map. (Film referenced: *Zan Boko*.)

Nikiema), his pregnant wife Nopoko (Colette Kaboré) and their two children, Talato and Tibo, live and work on their ancestral land. Nopoko and her midwife inform Tinga that her pregnancy may be difficult, and he must perform a water ritual to ward off danger.

After the ritual and the difficult birth of their third child, Tibilo, Nopoko and Tinga's family notice and observe the day-by-day transformation of their traditional use of farmland and the dwindling practices of agricultural life. The appearance of a new arriviste and wealthy family of five – a westernized mirror of Tinga's family – sets off a string of annoyances and humiliations. The Tougouri family resides in a large, two-storey villa residence built adjacent to and overlooking Tinga's compound. The noise of loudly recorded cool jazz played at a party keeps baby Tibilo awake at night. At his party, the neighbour Mr Tougouri, expresses a wish to acquire Tinga's compound to create a landscape and pool. Using his watchman as a go-between, the rich neighbour, egged on by his wife, makes repeated overtures to acquire the villagers' property and exerts increasing pressure on them to agree.

In one sequence, Nopoko is preparing soumbala sauce, a condiment similar to a protein- and mineral-rich mustard, made from fermented seeds of the fruit of the néré tree (African locust bean) common to the West Africa's savannah, which exudes a strong odour that attracts flies. A town official arrives in the compound and tells Nopoko that there have been complaints about the smell and the flies and that she risks being fined.

The director weaves a parallel narrative around broadcast media technologies, particularly television, and the efforts of an activist journalist, Yabre Tounsida (Célestine Zongo), to incite public outcry over the blatant injustice of land appropriation. He uses Tinga's story as the subject of a televised panel discussion. When Tinga arrives in the studio and is introduced and invited to speak on the panel set, the camera cuts to the modern interior of his influential neighbour's living room, where he and his wife have tuned in. The camera cuts to Tinga, and as he begins to tell his story – watched by the influential neighbour – the camera again cuts back to the neighbour and his wife, who recognizes the man whose land they usurped. Mr. Tougouri picks up his telephone and speaks to a powerful government official, and a message is relayed to the station ordering it to immediately take the show off the air. The 1980s television screen goes blank, and an announcer appears to present an alternative programme.

In 2014, architect Jean-Philippe Vassal participated in a post-screening discussion of *Zan Boko*, in which he described his experience in Niamey, Niger, where, in the early 1980s, he worked for five years as an urbanist in a small municipal planning team. He prefaced his remarks with an emphasis on the quality of life that he found in Niamey, which led him to stay on for four more years after his initial contract. In 1984, he and his partner Annie Lacaton, learning from local tradition, built a temporary first home of straw matting in Niamey (the structure was to last two years).[10]

At that time, a transition was taking place in Niamey. The municipality did not yet have an overall electricity network, paved roads or storm and sanitary sewage systems. Where once a local ruler would have allocated terrain in response to a request for land, it was now a municipal administration where Vassal worked that was responsible for creating, allocating and numbering urban plots. He also worked on the scale of the city as a whole. By the end of his five years there, the team had completed the *Schéma directeur d'urbanisme* or overall urban plan. Vassal also briefly mentions that, given the rapid growth of Ouagadougou, the location of Tinga's ancestral land would have been close to the centre of the city.[11]

Notes

1 Amadou T. Fofana, 'Sembène's *Borom Sarret:* A Griot's Narrative', *Literature/Film Quarterly* 39, no. 4 (2011): pp. 255–265 (p. 260) (accessed 15 December 2023) https://www.jstor.org/stable/43798800.

2 Michael Atkinson, 'Ousmane Sembène: We Are No Longer in the Era of Prophets', *Film Comment* 29, no. 4 (July–August 1993): pp. 63–64 (accessed 12 December 2023) https://www.filmcomment.com/article/ousmane-sembene-we-are-no-longer-in-the-era-of-prophets/.

3 Paulin Soumanou Vieyra, director, 'L'Envers du décor: Ousmane Sembène' ('Behind the Scenes: The Making of Ceddo'), Senegal, 1981, 25 min., starring Ousmane Sembène.   https://www.criterionchannel.com/behind-the-scenes-the-making-of-ceddo. See also: Ceddo (Outsiders), directed by Ousmane Sembène, produced by Filmi Domirev (Senegal) and the Ministère de la Coopération (France), https://www.youtube.com/watch?v=9ipcync79CI.

4 Ibid. See also: Malcolm Coad, 'Ousmane Sembene and *Ceddo*: With Excerpts from the Ceddo Film Script', *Index on Censorship* 10, no. 4 (1981): pp. 32–33 (accessed 12 December 2023) https://doi.org/10.1080/03064228108533236. Malcolm Coad's text includes several script extracts that help explain the narrative action. The ban is mentioned on page 32.

5 *Portail agroalimentair du Sénégal*, (website) n.d. (accessed 31 December 2023) https://www.agroalimentaire.sn/40-consommation-et-marche/.

6 Mabel Gundlach, *Saving Senegal's Peanut Basin*, D W (*Deutsche Welle*), 27 October 2015. 4 min. 51 sec (accessed 28 November 2023) (A short video on local collectives advocating ethical farming and being critical of monoculture industrial farming). Federal Ministry for the Environment, 'Nature Conservation, Building and Nuclear Safety', dw.com/globalideas, 2015. https://www.dw.com/en/global-ideas-soil-erosion-peanuts-senegal/a-18807107. See also: One World Award, Ibrahima Seck, silver, 2014 (accessed 28 September 2023) https://www.one-world-award.com/ibrahima-seck.html.

7 John D.H. Downing, 'Post-Tricolor African Cinema, Toward a Richer Vision', in *Cinema, Colonialism, Post Colonialism, Perspectives from the French and Francophone Worlds*, ed. Dina Sherzer. Austin: University of Texas Press, 1996. pp. 188–228 (p. 219).

8 Suzanne H. McRae, '*Yeelen* A Political Fable of the "Komo" Blacksmith /Sorcerers', *Research in African Literatures* 26, no. 3 (African Cinema Autumn 1995): pp. 57–66 (pp. 57–58) (accessed 10 August 2023) https://www.jstor.org/stable/3820136.

9 In 2023 Ougadougou's metro area population was 3,204,000, a 4.84% increase from 2022. In 1988, the metro area's population was 493,000 with a growth rate of 4.45 per cent. The metro area population of Ouagadougou in 1985 was 424,000, with a growth rate of 9.84 per cent (accessed 10 November 2023) https://www.macrotrends .net/cities/23192/ouagadougou/population.

10 Rowan Moore, 'Architects Anne Lacaton and Jean-Philippe Vassal on the Joy of Reusing Buildings Rather than Knocking them Down', *The Observer*, 10 December 2023 (accessed 10 December 2023) https://www.theguardian.com/artanddesign /2023/dec/10/anne-lacaton-and-jean-philippe-vassal-soane-medal. See also: The Soane Medal Lecture, 28 November 2023 (accessed 10 December 2023) https://www .soane.org/soane-medal/2023-lacaton-vassal.

11 Jean-Philippe Vassal, *Rencontre-Débat avec Jean-Philippe Vassal et Thierry Paquot, Cité de l'architecte et du patrimoine*. Paris, 12 November 2014 (accessed 10 November 2023) https://www.citedelarchitecture.fr/fr/video/zan-boko.

Chapter 2

MIGRATION SCENARIOS

Of all the great challenges facing Africa, in the beginning of this century, none is as urgent and as far-reaching as that of the mobility of its population.[1]

Achille Mbembe

Contemporary cinema remains highly engaged in migration narratives. The set of films in this chapter addresses demographic shifts, population growth, dispersion and migration scenarios within the African continent, between Africa and Europe and other nations and continents. Population mobility ranges from rural exodus to populations scattered by military conflict to climate change effects on territory, from drought to flooding to coastal erosion. Early films on migration tend to depict Europe as the desired destination. More recent films have been addressing African migration within the continent and beyond to other continents. In a context of ever-increasing reliance on extensive refugee camps, urbanists speculate that an impending intense rural urbanisation may take forms modelled after the various types of refugee camps.

Med Hondo, *Soleil Ô*, France/Mauritania, 1970, 98 Minutes

The director has transcribed his own experiences in a work of docufiction, in a process resembling autofiction, which, through the daily experiences and adventures of a Mauritanian in France and his responses and those of his acquaintances to French urban culture and mores, explores the complex range of French reactions to the mid-twentieth-century wave of African immigration to the nation.

The film derives much of its impact from the director's engagement with contemporary and radical theatre of the era. The opening sequences make use of satirical theatrical sketches, lampooning colonial regimes and religions, some set in studio black box contexts, others shot in open air. The arrival on the city scene of the main protagonist, Guadeloupan actor Robert Liensol, sets off an array of scenes that take place outside, on the streets and pavements of a French city, as he seeks white-collar employment as an accountant. In a variety of ways, he is rudely thrown out, brushed off and sent back into the street. This litany of rejections at a personal level opens onto scenes describing even more entrenched, systemic prejudice against the visible minority migrant, causing him to shed his illusions, as he realizes he has been misled by his initial identification with French culture.

Before entering the world of cinema and theatre, Mohamed Abid Medoun Hondo had worked in many jobs and particularly valued his time working in restaurants in Marseille, where he remembered learning the most about the dominant culture, whose values he trenchantly criticizes. His insights also came from his theatrical troupe, the Griot-Shango theatre, which he co-founded with Liensol in 1966. Many of the film scenes appear as if they might have been workshopped and rehearsed in Hondo's Montparnasse apartment to optimize their impact.[2] In the film, the protagonist's encounters with blue-collar workers are carefully differentiated, and their themes contrast with meeting more subtle racial prejudice from middle class and left-wing individuals and organizations. The scenes in which the protagonist socializes with a blonde, white Parisienne in a chic Etoile district drew attention in their street locations in the glares of disapproving passers-by, which underscore the sexual politics and the ensuing collision with the radical and revolutionary politics of the era.

A long sequence of surreal near madness in the setting of a forest, interrupted by a strange, infuriating encounter with a white nuclear family – they invite him to join them for a raucous meal at an outdoor table in front of their rural dwelling. This jarring, anti-social contact escalates the madness, causing the protagonist to bolt into the forest, building to a chaotic climax of the realization of the entrenched nature of the racism he has endured, and sends a closing message of radical awareness that action and revolutionary social re-education are the only sane paths forward.

Djibril Diop Mambéty, *Touki-Bouki* (*The Hyena's Journey*), Senegal, 1973, 88 Minutes

Dreams of leaving post-colonial Senegal to travel to Paris are shared by a disaffected couple, Mory (Magaye Niang), a young Zebu cattle herder, and Anta (Marème Niang), a university student and revolutionary, who propel the antic narrative of *The Hyena's Journey*, which is considered a quintessentially avant-garde film, shot on a minimal budget. The title's reference to the fearsome, carrion-feeding hyena predators – pack animals that smell the weakness of their prey and make laughing sounds as they track it down to its inescapable capture and feed on their downed prey while still alive – furnishes the director's analogy to the inevitability of corruption under capitalism.

The film opens with cattle roaming in a pastoral semi-arid landscape, with the camera zooming in on a younger boy, presumably Mori, herding cattle and comfortably riding a Zebu. The scene jump cuts to ghastly scenes of frightened, panicking cattle on the killing floor of the slaughterhouse.

The film's narrative veers between idyll to horror to a quasi-road movie, with the couple riding on a motorcycle adorned with Mory's iconic Zebu skull and horns.

The couple attempt a snatch-the-cashbox caper at a Senegalese wrestling match, which leads to an abandoned brutalist concrete seaside villa, not an uncommon coastal sight. The landscape prompts Mory to remember Charley, an amicable gay man (Ousseynou Diop), who entertains guests by the pool at his seaside villa. Mory and Anta drop by to improvise another comically absurd crime caper and abscond with suitcases trailing clothing, and a car and driver. The ensuing sequences drive and augment the fragmented narrative as Mory hesitates, changes his mind and veers away from the gangplank just as they are about to board the boat bound for France. The narrative fractures into a series of disconnected Port, city and roadside scenes, and Mory dreams a gloriously surreal solo nude parade sequence, referring back to an earlier parade sequence featuring close-ups of Mory and Anta dressed in fine new clothes in the back of a convertible, waving like royalty. At the end of the film, Anta, stultified with ennui, waits on deck in Dakar's port, having boarded the boat bound for France, and while waiting, listening to French passengers make disparaging remarks about the colonies, departs without Mory.

With the re-release of several of Mambéty's films, what was once considered a meagre output can be appreciated as an overarching arc of themes that address the city of Dakar, its population – especially the underprivileged – and its surrounding landscapes.

Mambéty's penultimate film, and the last released in his lifetime, *Hyènes* (*Hyenas*, 1992), plays out as a tragicomedy in which one of the protagonists, Linguère Ramatou (Ami Diakhate), seeks to wreak vengeance on her fickle lover, Dramaan Dramah (Mansour Diouf), with a macabre plan to humiliate and finally destroy the struggling village of Colobane – the name of Mambéty's home district in Dakar. Based on *The Visit of the Old Lady* (1956), a play by the Swiss playwright Friedrich Dürrenmatt, Mambéty's film develops a dark and lush version of the play's vengeful vision. An iron-willed older woman, once exiled from her town and obliged to make her way in life as a prostitute, returns from across the Atlantic to avenge the humiliations of her youth, demanding nothing less than the life of her former lover, Dramaan, who deserted her when she was pregnant to marry a wealthier woman. The flinty Linguère Ramatou can be interpreted as a metamorphosis of the young, striving Anta, now hell-bent on exacting revenge on the parallel character that Mory has become: charming, guileless and weak.

Now a rich woman, Linguère Ramatou declares herself to be richer than the International Monetary Fund, and schemes to win over the town's gullible population with staged giveaways of consumer items such as refrigerators and other household goods. There are memorable scenes which include Dramaan Dramah's wife, Madame Dramah (Faly Gueye), who signals from within the crowd, approaches and, as she reaches the stage, waves her arm over the display of appliances and demands to have it all. The film's closing scenes show a wide-open, empty, arid landscape and close-up shots of a crowd of Colobane's citizens pressing up against the once affable, now abject Dramaan Dramah, and when they draw back, as the camera draws back, he simply disappears.

In the final sequence, the script has added a last demolition and burial, as the camera pans over the utter destruction of the town, with bulldozers churning over the raw earth – only total obliteration will satisfy Linguère's all-consuming revenge.

Djibril Diop Mambéty's last film (shown posthumously) is part of his second trilogy, which he called *Histoires des petits gens* (Tales of Ordinary People) and is a bright, upbeat work, radiating with a hopeful vision of opportunities seized. *La Petite Vendeuse de Soleil* (*The Little Girl who Sold the Sun*, 1999) is a 45-minute film that defies the tropes of marginalization and exclusion and depicts the triumph of a significantly handicapped young girl, Sili Laam (Lissa Baléra), who fights for the right to earn her own living. Set in Dakar and in the port of Dakar, Sili's last name, Laam, suggests a link with low-caste tannery workers.[3] She finds her way from a peri-urban settlement, the *Cité des Tomates* near the airport, and asserts her right to work selling newspapers in a context where only boys sell papers on the street in Dakar. In this short narrative, the scenes of the city are aglow with promise. The Plateau's arcades with their newsagents, cafés and sidewalks gleam in the sunlight; the street can be a setting for the crisis of a woman driven mad but also holds possibilities of reward, and the disadvantaged gather to socialize, organize and defend themselves, while the Port is a bustling place of adventure.

Thomas Loubière, *Le Camp suspendu*, France/Chad, 2020, 70 Minutes

Time has stalled for the Central African refugees and Chadian returnee refugees who fled the 2013 civil war in the Central African Republic. Currently living in one of many camps in Chad, they lack the resources to leave and have remained in stasis for over a decade. Formerly known as Zarfaye, the camp lies along the road to Gaoui on the northeast outskirts of N'Djaména, the capital of Chad, with a population of 1 million, and the regionally strategic location of a French military airbase, Fort Lamy. Before fleeing the Central African Republic, most of the camp's occupants had been merchants and traders in Bangui, the capital, with a population of 1 million and the largest city of the Central African Republic. (See Figure 2.1.)

Thomas Loubière's documentary records life in the suburban camp and the overlong occupancy by Chadian returnees. The interviews with young people in the camp describe chilling memories of violent events during the 2013 conflict between Christians and Muslims in the Central African Republic. The camp's accommodation consists of long lines of rectangular white tents spread over a relentless Cartesian grid. A major theme in the documentary is how the occupants adapt to the tedium of daily life in a camp that offers little in the way of counselling, education or opportunity.

On a couple of occasions, the occupants are filmed staging semi-improvised theatrical skits, which recreate painful scenes of forced migration, eviction or rejection that sometimes elicited laughter at their own predicament as a way of dealing with uncomfortable realities over which they have no control.

Near the end of the documentary, the filmmakers interview camp occupants, who, backed by a humanitarian organization, had been allocated living quarters in N'Djaména and had been financed for a six-month trial stay and social re-insertion, but lack of opportunity, adequate funding and social support in the city exhausted their resources. They returned again to the camp, relieved to be back in a supportive community. The documentary, written by Loubière and Maud Rivière, is discreet, with almost no visible intervention on the part of the filming crew. Nor does the camera explore the city and surrounding landscape outside the camp, neither in N'Djaména nor the nearby town of Gaoui, known for its history, no doubt due to security issues.[4] Originally, the camp was intended to house refugees for under two months, at which point they were to be reintegrated with the local population. The film ends with the information that the average length of stay in a refugee camp is 17 years.

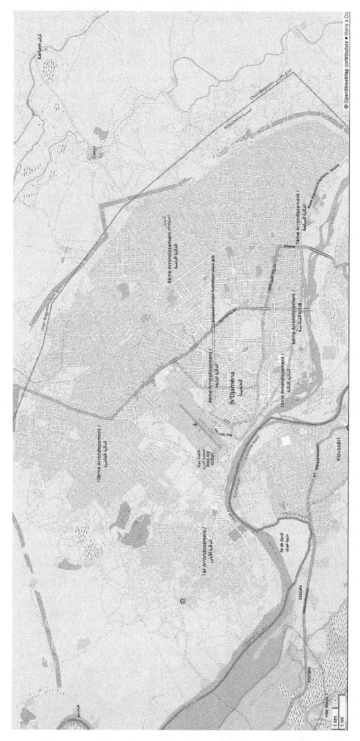

Figure 2.1 Chad, N'Djaména, courtesy Open Street Map. (Film referenced: *Le Camp Suspendu.*)

Ousmane Zoromé Samassékou, *The Last Shelter* (*Le dernier refuge*), France/Mali/South Africa, 2021, 86 Minutes

The Last Shelter is the second feature film by the Malian director Ousmane Zoromé Samassékou. Set in Mali at a migrant shelter, the Caritas Migrant House in Gao, the gateway city to the Sahara Desert, the documentary gives young migrants a voice to speak about their choice to leave their homelands, and the shelter also helps some to return home. (See Figure 2.2.)

The film opens with a warning to migrants who seek to reach other countries by traversing the Sahara: a team from the shelter is shown constructing gravestones and markers with the names and dates of birth in memory of those who stayed at the shelter – most often young migrants born in the mid-nineties – from Togo, Ivory Coast and Guinea – and who had died after attempting unsuccessfully to traverse the Sahara. At the time of filming, large numbers of migrants were traversing the city of Gao, Mali, a crossroads town with a population of 85,000 at the edge of the desert. Many migrants have stayed at the shelter, a sanctuary located along the multiple routes that converge in Gao, with shelter employees estimating the numbers running up to the thousands.

Two young girls, Esther (Esther Dorothée Safiatou) and Kady (Kadijatou Outtaro), arrive at the shelter. After being shown their room, they ask one another if this place can be trusted. When the shelter administrator, Eric Alain Kamdem, interviews them, Esther, stone-faced in her hijab with tears rolling down her cheek, refuses to give a cell number or any family information, except to mention that she has an aunt living in a small town in Burkina Faso.

During their stay, they befriend and encourage an older woman, Natacha (Natacha Akim), who has been living in a solitary state of suspension. Later, Esther Dorothée Safiatou confides some of her painful family memories to the camera, filmed in close-up, as she contemplates and narrates her life story. And an unnamed female shelter resident recounts even more disturbing stories of sexual exploitation, but not in front of the camera. While she speaks, the director pans over abandoned homes and vast landscapes in the unforgiving climate of the Sahel.

The psychological and medical support provided by the shelter is shown to be invaluable. Constantly arriving migrants often need treatment and receive basic medical care whether for worn-out feet or mental confusion and delusion.

By the end of the documentary, Esther has stubbornly held on to her plan to go to Algeria with Kady, declaring it will free her. She admits that she had always felt unloved by her mother, even as a child, and that she arrived in

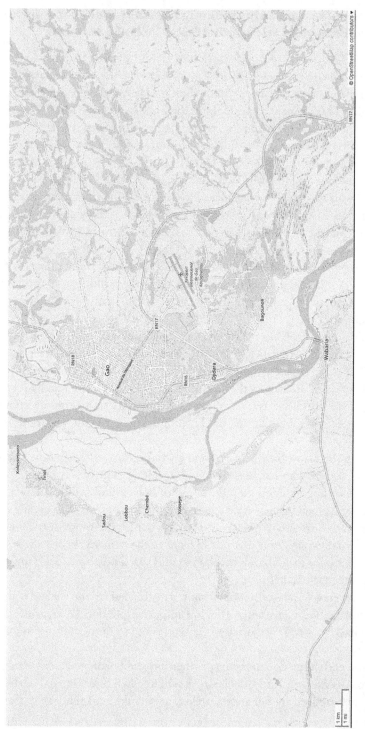

Figure 2.2 Mali, Gao, courtesy Open Street Map. (Film referenced: *The Last Shelter.*)

Gao full of anger. Staying at the shelter has unburdened her, but she and her friend still choose not to return to Burkina Faso. They depart in the night for Algeria.

Outside, young male shelter residents drink tea and discuss the challenges of traversing the Sahara Desert: the roadblocks, the payoffs that must be made to pass through them, the fake roadblocks, bandits and the possible routes through the desert.[5]

Marc Serena, *The Writer from a Country without Bookstores*, Spain, 2019, 79 Minutes

Marc Serena's documentary *The Writer from a Country without Bookstores*, follows the writer Juan Tomás Ávila Laurel during his return visit to Equatorial Guinea, a former Spanish colony. Originally from Annobón Island, the writer's native language is Annobonese (Annobonese Fa d'Ambu, a sort of Portuguese Creole) as well as Spanish, the lingua franca of Equatorial Guinea. He lived for most of his early life in Malabo, Equatorial Guinea's capital, where he studied and worked as a nurse. As a consequence of his much-publicized hunger strike in opposition to Equatorial Guinea's authoritarian regime, he became known as a dissident, was obliged to self-exile and has been living in Barcelona, Spain, since 2011. Because he has never claimed refugee status, he was able to return unhindered to Malabo, as he explains in an interview. There Serena filmed him chafing at the limitations of the static society oppressed by the long-enduring dictatorship and perpetually televisual presence of Teodoro Obiang Nguema Mbasogo, whose long-term project carves a new capital in the eastern rainforest. True to the film's title, the author meets up with playwrights and writers who pull their books out of knapsacks to show how they have to carry their publications with them. (See Figure 2.3.)

Laurel's visit coincided with the fortieth anniversary of the country's president, Obiang, the dictator who has ruled since 1979, and the writer appears profoundly uncomfortable as he watches bizarre, televised propaganda showing the despotic ruling family displaying costly cars and expensive playthings – a newspaper reported that Obiang's son, the country's first vice president, brings his jet-skis along with him in a spare super-yacht.[6]

While fundraising for the film, the director used the project title, *Guinea, el documental prohibido* (*Guinea, The Forbidden Documentary*), and it addresses the static, stunted and undeveloped character of the cultural sector of Guinean society rather than offering a literary analysis of the writer's work. In the film, he explains: 'I have written lots of books, most of them denouncing the situation in my country'. He turned his collection of stories into a novel that was translated into English from the Spanish manuscript and

Figure 2.3 Equatorial Guinea, Malabo, courtesy Open Street Map. (Film referenced: *The Writer from a Country without Bookstores*.)

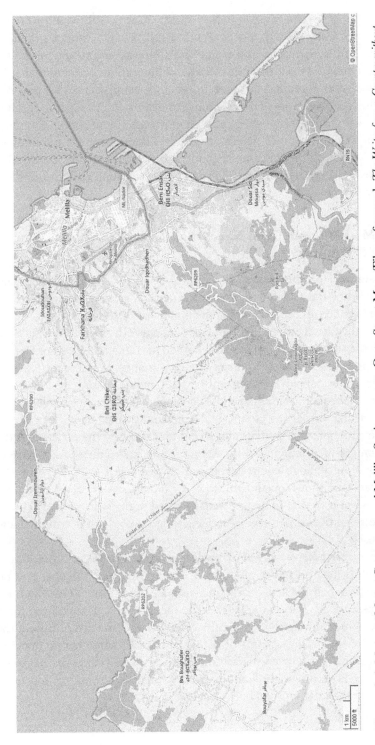

Figure 2.4 Morocco,Mount Gourougou and Melilla, Spain, courtesy Open Street Map. (Film referenced: *The Writer from a Country without Bookstores.*)

published as *The Guruguru Pledge* (And Other Stories, 2017) and in French as *Sur le mont Gourougou* (Asphalte Éditions, 2017). The autobiographical narrative of his alienation as a result of his migration journeys presented in the documentary parallels the first-hand biographical accounts that he researched and compiled in order to create a multi-voiced book of stories, told from the perspective of many migrants from Nigeria, Gambia or Mali, who at that time were camped in groups organized by their language in Mount Gurugu's forest. At just 10 kilometres from the Spanish enclave Melilla, it had become an informal migrant camp and gathering place for hundreds of African migrants seeking to jump the last hurdle to get to Spain.[7]

Hind Meddeb and Thim Naccache, *Paris Stalingrad*, France, 2019, 88 Minutes

In the summer of 2016, when the eradication of the extensive temporary camp known as the 'Calais jungle' was imminent, African migrants flocked to Paris and formed an urban camping site under the elevated Stalingrad metro line, near the Canal Saint-Martin in Paris's nineteenth arrondissement. Seen through the story of Souleymane Mohammad, a young refugee from Darfur, the documentary reveals the impact of large numbers of migrants living on the street. The narrative tracks daily events, making painfully visible the authorities' callous mishandling of the phenomenon. The camera follows and documents the surreal and often brutal behaviour by the officials sent to deal with the situation: the herding and round-up tactics by the police, and the sanitation crews' destroying of the encampment, under the shocked gaze of the director, neighbourhood residents and refugee youth.

Migrants are shown queuing in front of a building at 127 Boulevard de la Villette – where at that time they were required to register in order to begin the administrative process – only to have a sign posted at the entrance that read 'closed'.

Buses marked *bus de solidarité* (homeless assistance buses) are filmed pulling up while long queues of migrants living on the street, directed to wait, lined the pavements. Then, instead of assistance being given to each in turn, there was a triage. Those who had appointments were separated from those without. While small groups of local women organizers tried to inform the migrants of their rights, teams of police, almost all white males, imposed absurd rules, then hazmat-suited sanitation crews in bulldozers ploughed over and removed the light foam mattresses, meagre belongings and small tents where the migrants had been sleeping.

Souleymane is introduced as he roams the boulevards, and he recites one of his poems:

We are the exiles.
Silent with thousands of stories in our hearts, in life silence is golden.
    Don't be afraid of death, Life will come to you.
To survive, I will embark on an impossible quest.
If fate is against you, reply with a smile. Be the living proof that fate is
    different for everyone. That's life.
We are the exiles.

Souleyman also recounts his fear of descending into a narrow hole in the ground, at a time when he worked as a child labourer, in a gold mine in Libya.

The camera focusses on multitasking Agathe Nadimi, who explains the situation. She helps to provide food, a telephone and a place to sleep for a night. The film documents several incidents: one where the refugees hold a demonstration demanding their rights, another where the police and riot police surround, or 'kettle' the refugees in an area, and beside the waiting buses, hours pass in the rain before they are evacuated. The remaining refugees living on the street lose their sense of community and retreat to scattered street spaces.

The Stalingrad camp is dispersed, and fencing is placed around the sheltered area beneath the metro, which is reallocated as a playground. Ultimately, the migrants must apply at the *Office Français de la Protection des Réfugiés et Apatrides* (OFPRA, the French Office for the Protection of Refugees and Stateless Persons), and after a four-to-six-hour interview, they must wait for two months to find out if they are able to stay on and apply for papers.

Souleymane Mohammad turns out to be one of the lucky ones. He is filmed taking a train to a residence in Nancy, where he will wait for his papers. He is shown preparing a meal and chopping onions and chicken in the collective kitchen. Sometime after he receives his documents, he is seen working in an auto body shop, and for the first time in the documentary, he waves with a smile to the camera.

A co-editor for the journal *RightsViews*, Rowena Kosher, updates the narrative – Souleymane works in road-building and has been in touch with his mother by cell phone – and she recognizes the directors' engagement with the migrants, writing, 'As the refugee crisis continues in Paris, films like *Paris Stalingrad* provide important insight into a human rights issue largely hidden in the international conversation'. More importantly, this film recentres the 'human' in human rights. With dignity, agency and poetry, refugees tell their stories on their own terms.[8]

Figure 2.5 Algeria, Matares, Tipasa, courtesy: Open Street Map. (Film referenced: *Matares*.)

Rachid Benhadj, *Matares*, 2019, Algeria, 90 Minutes

The drama *Matares*, was shot on location among the Matares Roman ruins, near Tipasa, a coastal town in Algeria. The film depicts the journey of sub-Saharan Africans aiming to go to Italy but temporarily living in an Algerian refugee camp. An eight-year-old Catholic Ivorian child, Mona (Dorian Yohoo), encounters 10-year-old Saïd (Anis Salhi), a local Muslim boy. (See Figure 2.5.)

Mona resists the role of beggar assigned to her by the migrant smuggler Cedric, a threatening man who has promised to arrange a voyage to reunite her and her mother with her father in Italy. She hides her long, dark robe and explores the shore and the Roman ruins, finding a sepulchre where she can talk and be spiritually supported, praying with imagined and remembered friends and allies. She invents a more creative way to earn money, making daisy chain coronets of dandelions to sell to the affluent, carefree crowds of tourists visiting the ruins.

As Mona explores the Roman ruins, she happens upon a guide pointing to small stone coffin-shaped ruin fragments scattered in the landscape and informing tourists that Matares was a children's necropolis.

Mona shows outward poise in confronting her circumstances and composes an inner narrative heard in voiceover. She comforts herself by inventing a spiritual narrative, projecting a character called Adam and asking why Adam is insulted and bullied.

The two children, Mona and Saïd, clash at their first encounter. Saïd, a bold daredevil, perceives her as competing on his territory for tourist custom. The children eventually become friends and unite in a struggle against the adults, who seek to exploit and abuse them. One day, Mona disappears, and when Saïd seeks her out in the tents that housed her, her mother and the other immigrants, he is told that the group has been dispersed.[9]

A black-and-white documentary montage brackets the film, commemorating the tragic events that took place in Algeria two years earlier, when some 13,000 African migrants were left without water or food at the edge of the Sahara Desert.[10]

Notes

1 Achille Membe, *Brutalism*. Trans. Stephen Corcoran. Durham, NC: Duke University Press, 2024, p. 97. Originally published in French as *Brutalisme*. Paris: La Découverte, 2020, p. 154, 'De tous les grands défies auxquels l'Afrique fait face en ce début de siècle, aucun n'est aussi urgent et aussi lourd de conséquences que la mobilité de sa population'.

2 Françoise Pfaff, 'The Films of Med Hondo, an African Filmmaker in Paris', *Jump Cut* no. 31 (March 1986): pp. 44–46 (accessed 15 December 2023) https://www.ejumpcut

.org/archive/onlinessays/JC31folder/HondoFilms.html. See also: Some film crit-ics see parallels with work in a collective, in the L.A. Rebellion filmmakers of the 1960s and 1970s, that included Charles Burnett, Julie Dash, Haile Gerima and oth-ers. David Hudson, 'LA Rebellion at LEFFEST', *The Daily, Criterion*, 8 November 2022. https://www.criterion.com/current/posts/7985-la-rebellion-at-leffest. Richard Brody, 'Med Hondo's Vital Political Cinema Comes to New York', *New Yorker*, 20 March 2024 (accessed 12 May 2024) https://www.newyorker.com/culture/the-front-row/med-hondos-vital-political-cinema-comes-to-new-york.

3 California Newsreel, '*Le Franc* and *La Petite Vendeuse de soleil*, Notes for Viewing the films', (accessed 10 October 2023) https://newsreel.org/guides/francpetite.htm.

4 Manuel Herz, 'Refugee Camps in Chad: Planning Strategies and the 2007 UN High Commissioner for Refugees', (accessed 12 November 2023). https://www.unhcr.org/sites/default/files/legacy-pdf/4766518f2.pdf. The report by Manuel Herz mentions the security issues and the undefined, uncentred urban character of N'Djaména of a decade before.

5 Ousmane Zoromé Samassékou, director, 'Film Talk: *The Last Shelter*', in a panel discussion with Sonja Hövelmann, after the film's première at the Human Rights Film Festival Berlin, 2021, 37 min (accessed 10 October 2023) https://www.youtube.com/watch?v=hK8FFUok82w. See also, Complete featured films, *The Last Shelter*. Generation Africa, n.d. (accessed 10 October 2023) https://www.generationafrica.co.za/films/the-last-shelter-featured/ and Jessica Kiang, 'The Last Shelter', Review: Scenes From a Rest-Stop on a Migrant Route Across Africa, 30 April 2021 (accessed 10 October 2023) https://variety.com/2021/film/reviews/the-last-shelter-review-1234962677/.

6 Michael M. Phillips, 'The Dictator's Son Wanted his Yacht Back […]', *Wall Street Journal*, 6 May 2024. On the yachts of vice president of Equatorial Guinea, Teodorin Nguema Obiang Mangue (accessed 20 June 2024) https://www.wsj.com/wolrd/africa/yacht-oilworkers-equatorial-guinea-hostages-36ee8677.

7 Juan Tomás Ávila Laurel, '*The Gurugu Pledge* and Diversity in the Narrative Voice', interview with Tobias Carroll, Trans. Jethro Soutar, *Words without Borders*, 10 January 2018 (accessed 11 October 2023) https://wordswithoutborders.org/read/article/2018-01/juan-tomas-avila-laurel-on-the-gurugu-pledge-and-diversity-in-the-narrative/.

8 Rowena Kosher, co-editor, 'A Refugee Crisis, Poetry, and a Camera: *Paris Stalingrad* Film Screening', *RightsViews*, 7 December 2020 (accessed 14 May 2024) https://blogs.cuit.columbia.edu/rightsviews/2020/12/07/a-refugee-crisis-poetry-and-a-camera-paris-stalingrad-film-screening/.

9 *Matares*, directed by Rachid Benhadj (Nour Films, Algeria, 2019, 90 min). can be streamed on Tubitv.com.

10 Lori Hinnant, 'Walk or die: Algeria Strands 13,000 Migrants in the Sahara', *AP News*, 25 June 2018, with contributions by Adoum Moussa and Tcherno Abarchi (accessed 12 May 2024) https://apnews.com/article/deserts-niger-africa-international-news-algeria-9ca5592217aa4acd836b9ee091ebfc20. See also: Elian Peltier, 'When a Tale of Migration is Not Just Fiction', *New York Times*, 18 May 2024. Photographs by Annika Hammerschlag, Reporting from a movie screening in Guèdiawaye, a suburb of Dakar, Senegal. *The New York Times*, 18 May 2024 (accessed 29 May 2024). A cau-tionary tale of migration, The film, *Io Capitano*, directed by Matteo Garrone, (2023) was projected in various locations in Senegal. https://www.nytimes.com/2024/05/18/world/africa/senegal-io-capitano-migration.html.

Chapter 3

URBANIZATION, INFRASTRUCTURE AND LANDSCAPE

Through contemporary African films and documentaries that draw attention to and explore a range of urban and rural infrastructures, this chapter addresses the phenomena of African urbanization and shifting landscapes due to modern mining territories of extraction, megaprojects, new cities, megacities, as well as unplanned cityscapes and informal settlements. In the face of climate change and, in some cases, to obtain more socio-political control, a range of global, private and public organizations have launched proposals for new kinds of cities and modes of urbanization, from top-down to grassroots. There is abundant literature regarding the rapid and imminent urbanization on the African continent and a recent economic report by the consultants McKinsey & Company predicts significant urban development everywhere on the continent, which at a macro scale, suggests that it would be well-advised to develop policies to encourage a more robust network of secondary cities.[1]

At the other end of macro-scale economic growth is the parallel incremental growth of dense informal settlements, which lack a corresponding infrastructure. The compressed scales of informal settlements often become microcosmic worlds within a city, as in the case of Kibera in Nairobi, Kenya, the largest of over one hundred informal settlements in Nairobi. Their issues of water supply and drainage are found in these kinds of settlements throughout Africa. This topic is introduced with a very short, succinct film, a microfilm that condenses the water and drainage concerns into a sound and image bite.

Idrissou Mora-Kpaï, *Arlit: Deuxième Paris*, Niger/France, 2004, 98 Minutes

The documentary *Arlit: Deuxième Paris* explores the environmental and health struggles resulting from uranium extraction in industrial sites near Arlit, a desert town in Niger. In interviews, the inhabitants of the region give first-hand accounts of an industrialized mineral resource extraction process which they perceive as incomprehensible, menacing and incongruous with their traditional way of life, one that has blighted their health and left indelible, destructive after-effects on the desert landscape, on Arlit and on other similarly exploited Tuareg towns in the region. (See Figure 3.1.)

The film opens with a dusty bus traversing a desert landscape and arriving at a mine site to drop off workers wearing deep blue boiler suits, who crowd at a wicket gate to the mine's entrance, next to a sign that reads, SOMAIR (Somair Arlit-Société des Mines de l'Aïr) Arlit. The camera then pans over to vast grey excavated and unprotected rock piles. Aerial views reveal the immense excavated landscape of the mine facilities, coated in pale, sandy dust. Arlit and Akokan, near the Aïr Mountain foothills, were mining towns where uranium was open-pit extracted from the local sandstone, then processed underground on site.

A Tuareg interviewee in voiceover states, 'We've no idea what they do in the facilities. We're not sure, but we've heard they remove stones from the sand and send them somewhere else'. Later in the film, at 40 minutes, two retired Tuareg men discuss their jobs, saying, 'When we started to work, we were told we'd be extracting something called uranium. We didn't know what it was. We still don't, really. We just extract it – or that it could make you sick'.[2]

They recount that since they were not very well informed about radioactivity, they did not, for example, change clothes after work to reduce the spread of dust when they were with their children. Another worker recalled that the yearly medical check-up was always positive, even when a worker subsequently became ill. An interview with the company doctor confirms this withholding of information. He stated that few workers were diagnosed with mine-induced silicosis or radioactive illness. Mine workers' illnesses were blamed on other diseases, such as smoking-related diseases and AIDS.

Later documentaries have also criticized the mine operations. A 54-minute film *La colère dans le vent* (*Anger in the Wind*, 2016 Niger/Benin/France), directed by Amina Weira (who was born in Arlit), relies on the experience of her father, a former mine worker, and emphasizes the damage caused by periodic dust storms that disperse radioactive dust.[3]

These issues have been much discussed by scholars and mining experts who have signalled similar concerns in events such as the presentation, 'What happens after mines close? The case of Uranium mine closure in Niger' – held at King's College London, 31 January 2023.[4] The closure of the Areva Corporation's subsidiary mining company COMINAK (Compagnie minière d'Akouta) in 2021, after having operated in the uranium mining industry for 45 years, precludes any possible reparations. The original French companies

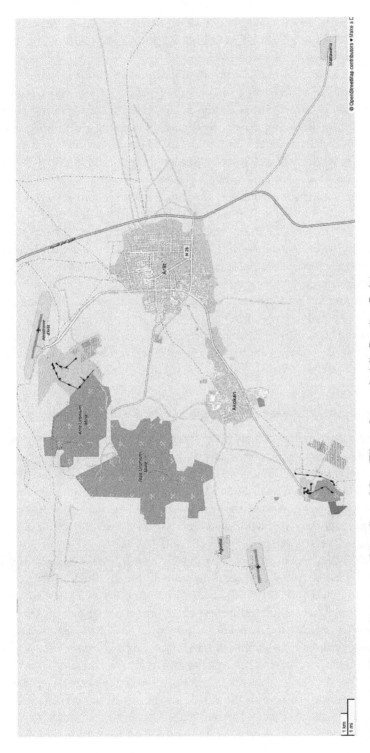

Figure 3.1 Niger, Arlit, courtesy Open Street Map. (Film referenced: *Arlit, Deuxième Paris.*)

have been replaced with new entities with different names, and Areva, which was refinanced and rebranded as Orano, continues to be blamed for lax environmental policies in the region.

Meanwhile, in the context of local political unrest and insecurity, France has diversified its sources of uranium. In the last decade, Niger accounts for about 20 per cent of France's uranium supply for its 56 operating nuclear reactors. There were angry reactions against France at a demonstration in Niamey on 3 August 2023: 'Fifty years that France exploits our uranium, enough is enough', said a 27-year-old student, Salim Sidimou, to a *New York Times* journalist reporting the event in Niamey.[5]

The nuclear industry in France is identified and branded as a well-funded, highly competent advanced technology industry – in marked contrast to the decrepit uranium mining industry in Arlit. The mining industry appears to destroy landscapes with impunity, and there are few tools available to hold international corporations accountable for ravaging a landscape and ignoring a local ecology in the search for extracted profit.

Condemnation and criticism of the future operation of the Imouraren mine, about 80 kilometres north of Arlit, are expressed in many articles, publications and blogs by investigative journalists. Uranium mining in Mounana, Gabon, has also raised concerns and is recorded in documentaries such as *Uranium, l'héritage empoisonné* (2009) by Dominique Hennequin.[6]

Mo Scarpelli, *Anbessa*, Ethiopia/Italy, 2019, 86 Minutes

Anbessa is a documentary filmed over several years, when extensive new multistorey housing was being built on farmland at the city edge of Addis Ababa. It focusses on the realities of unequal housing distribution and displacement as a side effect of rapid urbanization. An ambitious social housing programme forced the farmers and rural dwellers to relocate when the new apartments were built, and they were left to squat in makeshift dwellings and live in precarious situations on the peripheries of Addis Ababa.

Mo Scarpelli has been documenting the family, Asalif Tewold and his mother, for five years, and the narrative unfolds through the imaginative play of Asalif, a gifted child of 10, who lives with his mother in an ad hoc garden shed after they were displaced from their farmland a year before. Their surroundings contrast with the nearby construction site of the largest array of apartment complexes to be built in East Africa and the derisory radio advertising of the developers that the complex would be a 'sustainable community development that helps everyone'. There is incongruity here, given that this territory – Axum – was once the axis of a major trade network between the African continent, Arabia and Indian states.

Asalif hears the cries of a prowling hyena at night and imagines himself as a lion (anbessa in Amharic: the Lion of Judah is the national symbol of Ethiopia). During the day, he fashions a lion's mane headdress to wear and acts out a lion's roar. At night, in the shed, there is no light, no electricity and no real door which is a piece of scrap corrugated metal pulled across the doorway at night. Asalif is fascinated by wires, electrical parts and components, and scavenges through waste for discarded, usable parts. He puts together a flashlight and invents myriad small electrical items to improve life in their improvised home, amazing his mother at how easily he assembles helpful electrical items to ease their circumstances. But she also worries about his wanderings through the construction sites.

When Asalif meets and befriends a boy, who lives in a new apartment unit, and who invites him inside, the camera moves in for a close-up to show Asalif's face and eyes, fascinated in the glow of the boy's video game on a cell phone and his large flatscreen. Soon he is shown to be fabricating and showing off his more advanced self-made toys such as a helicopter with battery-run whirling blades.

In 2006, Ethiopia launched an ambitious building programme that included the construction of 500,000 apartment units, typically in the form of five- to six-storey blocks in a standard building type, and aimed to keep pace with the rapid urban growth in a country that had once been one of the least urbanized African countries. Mo Scarpelli recognized the social impact of this dramatic urbanization, which was the impetus for making the documentary:

> Once I was flying into Addis Ababa and I saw this massive condominium complex spanning the city [...] All over the world there are these massive condominiums, and this move into a modern structured lifestyle for all expanding cities. But I'd never in Ethiopia seen it be this vast, and Ethiopia historically has been very resistant to Westernisation.[7]

In 2022, the director posted an update on Anbessa, when she interviewed 16-year-old Asalif in Addis Ababa. He and his mother now live in more adequate lodgings, and he is shown busy mending a cell phone. He has reached grade nine and can support his mother by repairing electronics such as cell phones and tablets and mentions with pride that he has many customers.

He talks of his plans for the future. He would like to become an astronomer. At school, he has learnt about the galaxy and the history of astronomy in Ethiopia's Axumite Kingdom. And in the ancient Ethiopian city of Axum, an image of Jupiter is carved on its tallest obelisk, the Obelisk of Axum, a monolithic phonolite stele. He adds that in Lalibela, a historic town in the Amhara region, one of the passageways connecting the rock-hewn churches is carved with an image of Orion, further attesting to ancient knowledge of astronomy, in which – to paraphrase Asalif, Ethiopia was number one in astronomy and Egypt number two.[8]

Hassen Ferhani, *143 rue de désert* (*143 Desert Street*), Algeria/France/Qatar, 2020, 100 Minutes

Set in the southern Algerian desert, the film *143 rue du désert* has been described by several critics as a static road movie. Shot along Algerian Trans Saharan Highway 1 (Route National 1RN1), which bisects the Algerian Sahara, the film blends together documentary and scripted scenes, which laconically depict a mostly transient community and a traditional desert wayside stop run by a lone older woman called Malika. The director gives shape to a scenario of a small, authentic local business facing the impending transformation and modernization of the vast desert territory in the form of the construction of a large, modern petrol station and a hypermarché (a big box-style supermarket) that threatens to swallow it up.

Ferhani learnt of Malika's station-stop café from the novel *Nationale 1* (Casbah, 1999) by his friend Chawkwi Amari, who wrote about his stop there and his encounter with a group of falconers who sat calmly with their falcons. Interviews with Ferhani reveal a few of the sleight-of-hand techniques he used to integrate slice-of-life observation with movie-script fragments. Every day, the director drove 70 kilometres to the location for filming on the short month-and-a-half daily shoot, then worked for two months on sound editing, while construction of a large hypermarket and modern gas station continued nearby – a looming threat to Malika's simple two-room café.

The lone one storey simple building sometimes serves as a cinematic device. As the camera circumnavigates the building, it is a mute shelter, protruding out of the sand. Inside the main room of 20 square metres, there is little space for long pans and zooms. Except for a quick view of the kitchen, Malika's secrets are not revealed, nor is how she obtains water or how supplies are delivered. These practical subjects are not broached. But the simple front doorway with the view towards the road sometimes becomes a cinematic screen, and even a small side-order window serves as a tiny stage for a micro play, with the actor Samir El Hakim taking a scripted-role.[9]

The film emphasizes a sense of community values and belonging despite the transient nature of Malika's customers. As for spontaneity and happenstance, little is ordinary in such a place. There is a flow of visitors from various walks of life, and there are scenes of the café filled with a group of travelling folk musicians and Malika joining in the dance quite joyfully. At another point, the unannounced arrival of Maya, a Polish woman travelling alone on a motorcycle, piques Malika's curiosity. As Maya takes a seat next to her at the café table, Malika appraises her and her total autonomy on her lengthy road trip around the world. Two independent women sit side by side, but Malika finds her too much like a man. When the film was released in Poland, it turned out that Maya is a film producer and she attended the screening. Malika too attended the film's première in Algiers. She said, 'It's my film'.

Arie and Chuko Esiri, *Eyimofe* (*This Is My Desire*), Nigeria, 2020, 116 Minutes

> A city in a state of shifting impermanence. A place still becoming. In newer Lagos, houses sprout up on land reclaimed from the sea, and in older Lagos, buildings are knocked down so that ambitious new ones might live. A street last seen six months ago is different today, sometimes imperceptibly so – a tiny store has appeared at a corner – and sometimes baldly so, with a structure gone, or shuttered, or expanded. Shops come and go (Chimamanda Ngozi Adichie).[10]

Eyimofe (*This is My Desire*) is a dramatic debut feature film, set in Lagos and shot in 16 mm film, by directors who are twin brothers (twins are a common phenomenon, with a probability of one in ten in Yoruba culture). The story presents two parallel narratives about dreams to emigrate to Spain and Italy in the adjacent and parallel stories of Mofe (Jude Akuwudike), a senior factory electrical engineer, living through the aftermath of a fatal family accident due to a defective generator, and Rosa (Temioluwa Ami-Williams), a hairdresser. She looks out for her sister, Grace (Cynthia Ebijie), a pregnant teen sent by their mother to live with her in Lagos. The characters live in almost adjacent buildings in the same neighbourhood and sometimes share the same moment at a kiosk. To lend authenticity and to develop the local narrative, the scriptwriter, Chuko Esiri, rented an apartment in the Mushin district, which became the setting for the flat shared by Mofe and his sister's family. The curving axis of the Main Mushin Market, swarming with its constantly moving crowds, is prominently featured in aerial views when Rosa goes there to sell her cosmetics collection in order to purchase Grace's medicine. The narrative's maze-like intertwining of moments and situations, temporal intervals and geographic space are labyrinths shared by the characters: when Rosa arrives at the hospital, she passes just behind Mofe, who is at the reception counter with his supportive friend Abu (Charles Ukpong), and later Grace sits at Mofe's kiosk while he repairs her refrigerator (See Figure 3.2).

Both of the two main characters wish for and make plans to leave Lagos, and both are working two jobs. While grieving the loss of his sister and her

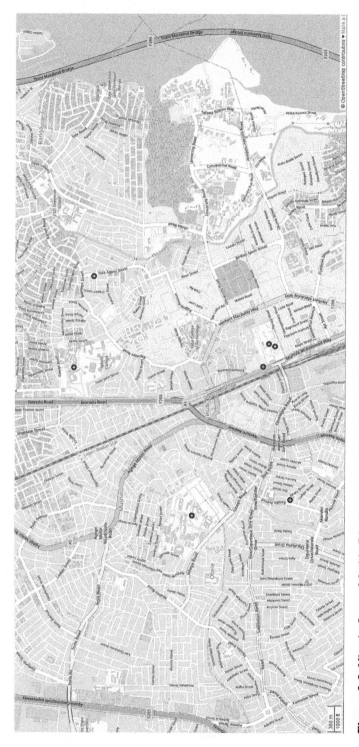

Figure 3.2 Nigeria, Lagos, Mushin District, courtesy Open Street Map. (Film referenced: *Eyimofe* (*This is My Desire*)).

children, Mofe shows patience, resignation and determination as he slowly navigates the labyrinthine paperwork and legal perils of extended families. Rosa meets a new boyfriend, Peter (Jacob Alexander), while working at a bar at night; by day she works in a pink-collar world at the hairdressing salon. She visits new kinds of places, such as a rooftop café with panoramic views of the megalopolis skyline, with her Lebanese-American boyfriend, but his affluent Lagosian friends sneer at her working-class financial worries. Mofe is fired from his job at a dilapidated printing factory as a senior electrical engineer, where he despaired of repairing a main electrical panel that was so overloaded that it looked like a plate of noodles. In another overlap of the two protagonists' lives, Mofe works nights as a security guard in the same luxury residential building where Rosa goes to meet Mama Esther (Chioma 'Chigul' Omeruah) – in her apartment, the woman who is interested in trading a trip to Italy for the prospect of Grace's unborn child.[11]

The double narrative weaves into the labyrinthine background of the Mushin District's street life, with overhead shots of its crowded, intensely colourful market and contrasts with glimpses of the tasteful, prosperous worlds in Lagos – space, luxury flats and skyscrapers, sometimes as distant and unattainable as Mofe and Rosa's hazy dreams of Europe.

To carry out their plans to leave Lagos, both protagonists have to moonlight to pay extortionate fees for false papers and passage. In each case, they are hit with financial setbacks, and their dreams of leaving are shelved. After the tragic loss of his sister Precious (Omoye Uzamere) and his nephews, Mofe struggles to pay hospital, morgue and funeral bills as well as probate on his sister's estate, only to have his father Jakpor (Sadiq Daba) lodge a legal claim as the rightful heir to his daughter's estate. Rosa must barter her sister's unborn child, but Grace's medical bills leave her with no money to pay her rent until she is left with an offer to marry the kindly landlord, Mr Vincent (Toyin Oshinaike), which, for her, is an option as unwanted as staying in Lagos.

The film paints a vivid picture of metropolitan greed and corruption and pinpoints aspects of illegal immigration: the open and unchecked manufacture of false documents and child trafficking in exchange for a passage to Europe. The role of the unctuous trafficker Mama Esther is richly played by the actor and comedian Chioma Omeruah, best known as Chigul.

When their dreams of life anew in Spain and Italy dissolve, Mofe and Rosa find comfort in the goodness of some of the secondary characters and in the compromises they have had to make in the bustling, densely packed and lively Mushin district.

In an epilogue, Mofe's plan to emigrate to Spain gradually fades. He rents a kiosk from his landlord, Mr Vincent, Rosa's suitor. Mofe engages in growing a business with Wisdom (Fortune Nwafor), his apprentice electrician. There is a sense of a new beginning at home in the mega-metropolis of Lagos.

Streamed Video and Screen Media: The Improvised Informal City

Raindrops (2019) is a three-minute short micro-film directed by Stephen Okoth Ochieng (also known as Ondivow). Set in Nairobi's Kibera, the film dramatizes the multiple leaks in the makeshift dwelling and home to Mitchel and the younger Angel in Kibera during the November rainy season. Kibera's landscape issues during the rainy season are seen and heard as dripping and pooling sounds, along with the coughing of the two young siblings in the home. The younger child, Angel, contracts pneumonia. The story reaches a climax with a visit to a medical clinic, and she recovers, but the film emphasizes the serious effects of illnesses that occur from water contamination. *Raindrops* was a finalist and received a special mention in the microfiction category of the 2019–2020 We Art Water Film Festival 5.[12]

Flooding, drought, drainage and clean water are landscape problems that arise from the specific topography and urban situation of informal settlements such as Kibera, Nairobi, Kenya, which is bisected by a riverbed that is usually dry except in the rainy season when it floods uncontrolled. NGOs (non-governmental organizations) and non-profit landscape design companies, such as Kounkuey Design Initiative, or KDI, based in Los Angeles and Nairobi, have published explanatory videos to disseminate their design solutions, with realistic examples of built projects and landscape interventions that address Kibera's landscape problems.[13]

KDI is engaged in a long-term series of undertakings and interactive discussions with the inhabitants for the Kibera Public Space Project, or Public Space Project Network, to improve Kibera's landscape, infrastructure and architecture. Their interventions already include 11 sites with new climate-resilient public spaces with sanitation and community centres, including the setting up of seven donated hand-washing stations during the pandemic, and the construction in 2019 of a pedestrian bridge across the Ngong River that runs through the settlement, to create a cohesive programme of 'community-responsive adaptation' to seasonal flooding. More information about these initiatives can be found in streamed presentations posted on social media sites such as X (formerly Twitter) and YouTube, and not least, those carried out through the United Nations Office (UNON), the UN's African headquarters in Nairobi, and UNESCO's Science, Technology and Innovation hub for Sub-Saharan Africa.[14]

Kibera's informal settlement has provided an alluring location for crime- and gangland-themed movies. A well-known crime chase film, *Nairobi Half Life* (2012), directed by David 'Tosh' Gitonga, was a product of a One Fine Day workshop, held by director Tom Tykwer in Nairobi. It combines familiar narratives of the double life of crime, a play within a play, and a desperate chase scene modelled on Tykwer's 1998 German crime thriller, *Run Lola Run*. Joseph Wairimu stars as Mwas, the naïve protagonist, who sells DVDs and performs in his hometown by reenacting the dialogue from wide-release action films. Mwas leaves his village for the metropolis of Nairobi, in the hope of becoming an actor, only to find himself swiftly jailed and then also as soon released and improbably cast in a robbery-themed play. The positive audience reaction to *Nairobi Half Life* was largely due to the technical brilliance of the sophisticated camera work, as well as the reference to daily life in Kibera, such as a scene where Mwas poses as the driver of a local vehicle, a *mkokoteni*, or open-wheeled cart, and outwits the police.

Gitonga's film was not just supported by the One Fine Day Films workshop in Nairobi, its narrative and cinematic techniques were well received by film critics as shaped by European film – *Run Lola Run* in particular. In 2019, the Goethe Institute reported that the workshops given by One Fine Day Films, a project begun in 2008 by Berlin-based director Tom Tykwer, have been involved in supporting some 1,000 filmmakers from 21 African countries.[15]

As for the informal city as a mode of urbanisation, according to the theorist AbdouMaliq Simone, it is timely and worthwhile to acknowledge and celebrate the tangible qualities of the improvised city as 'extending the understanding of the urban'.[16] Risk expert researchers continue to seek ways to integrate and regularize self-built settlements.[17]

Notes

1 Mayowa Kuyoro, et al., ed. Stephanie Strom, 'Reimagining Economic Growth in Africa: Turning Diversity into Opportunity', *McKinsey Global Institute*, 2023, p. 7 (accessed 5 June 2023) https://www.mckinsey.com/mgi/our-research/reimagining -economic-growth-in-africa-turning-diversity-into-opportunity.

2 *Arlit: Deuxième Paris*, directed by Idrissou Mora-Kpaï (MKJ Films, Niger/France, Noble Films, Benin, 2004, 98 min., quote at 40 min) (accessed 30 December 2023) See also: https://mubi.com/films/arlit-deuxieme-paris https://newsreel.org/video/ arlit-deuxieme-paris and https://video.alexanderstreet.com/watch/arlit-deuxieme -paris.

3 *La colère dans le vent*, (*Anger in the Wind*), directed by Amina Weira, (Vrai Vrai Films, Niger /Benin /France, 2016, 54 min) (accessed 12 December 2023) https://vraivrai -films.fr/la_colere_dans_le_vent.

4 Dr. Penda Diallo, et al., 'What Happens after Mines Close? The Case of Uranium Mine Closure in Niger', *King's College London*, 31 January 2023 (accessed 12 December

2023) https://www.kcl.ac.uk/events/what-happens-after-mines-close-uranium-mine
-closure-in-niger.

5 Salim Sidimou, student, quoting, in an article by Elian Peltier, 'A Shrinking Footprint
in Africa for France, the Former Colonizer That Stayed', *New York Times*, 6 August
2023. (with contributions by Declan Walsh reporting from Nairobi, Kenya, and
Omar Hama Saley from Niamey, Niger, as reported by journalists on Thursday Aug
2023 at a protest in Niamey, Niger's capital) (accessed 12 October 2023) https://www
.nytimes.com/2023/08/05/world/africa/niger-coup-france-west-africa.html.

6 Lucas Destrijcker and Mahadi Diouara, 'A Forgotten Community: The Little Town
in Niger Keeping the Lights on in France', *African Arguments*, 18 July 2017 (accessed
11 November 2023) https://africanarguments.org/2017/07/a-forgotten-community
-the-little-town-in-niger-keeping-the-lights-on-in-france-uranium-arlit-areva/.   See
also: *Uranium, l'héritage empoisonné*, directed by Dominique Hennequin (Film by Public
Sénat TV Channel, France, 2009), 52 min. and: Bertrand d'Armagnac, 'Uranium,
l'héritage empoisonné', *Le Monde*, 12 December 2009 (accessed 12 December 2023)
https://www.lemonde.fr/vous/article/2009/12/12/uranium-l-heritage-empoisonne
_1279679_3238.html. See also: Zeenat Hansrod, 'French Uranium Mine Leaves 20
million Tonnes of Radioactive Waste in Niger', 24 January 2023 (accessed 23 May
2024) https://www.rfi.fr/en/africa/20230124-french-uranium-miner-leaves-20-mil-
lion-tonnes-of-radioactive-waste-in-niger. Julie Pietri, 'Au Niger, une entreprise française a laissé 20 millions de tonnes de déchets radioactifs à l'air libre', *France Inter*,
23 January 2023 (accessed 23 May 2024) https://www.radiofrance.fr/franceinter/au
-niger-les-centrales-francaises-ont-laisse-20-millions-de-tonnes-de-dechets-radioac-
tifs-a-l-air-libre-2593286. 'Niger : fin de la production d'uranium à la Cominak, filiale
d'Orano', *Africa News*, 31 March, 2021. La Compagnie minière d'Akouta (Cominak),
une des deux filiales nigériennes du géant nucléaire français Orano (ex-Areva), a
annoncé mercredi l'arrêt définitif de sa production d'uranium dans le pays (accessed
20 June 2024) https://www.youtube.com/watch?v=WpKz1XPHC7I.

7 In Caitlin Quinlan's, 'Truth versus Progress: Mo Scarpelli on Anbessa, her Creative
Portrait of a Creative Ethiopian', *Sight and Sound Magazine*, 13 March 2019 (accessed 19
August 2023) https://www2.bfi.org.uk/news-opinion/sight-sound-magazine/inter-
views/mo-scarpelli-anbessa-documentary-asalif-ethiopia-development-truth-pro-
gress. See also: CITI, 'Ethiopia's Radical Redesign for Relentless Urban Growth',
CIT/IO, 6 December 2017 (accessed 10 October 2023) https://citi.io/2017/12/06/
ethiopias-radical-redesign-for-relentless-urban-growth/. Tom Gardner, 'Addis has
Run Out of Space': Ethiopia's Radical Redesign', photographs by Charlie Rosser,
The Guardian, 4 December 2017 (accessed 10 October 2023) https://www.theguardian
.com/cities/2017/dec/04/addis-ababa-ethiopia-redesign-housing-project.

8 Mo Scarpelli, '*Anbessa*, Update with Asalif, 2022', Rake Films (accessed 19 August
2023) https://vimeo.com/718096386. See also: additional information and press kit:
Anbessa https://www.imdb.com/title/tt7601098/ https://lightdox.com/wp-content/
uploads/2020/08/presskit-anbessa-2020.pdf.

9 Hassen Ferhani, director, 'A Conversation about *143 rue de désert*, with the director and
Madeleine Dobie', Maison Française, Columbia University, 13 April 2021 (accessed
19 August 2023) https://m.facebook.com/columbia.maisonfrancaise/videos/director
-hassen-ferhani-in-conversation-about-143-rue-du-d%C3%A9sert-with-madeleine-d
/3974578262638473/.

10 Chimamanda Ngozi Adichie, 'Still Becoming: At Home In Lagos With Chimamanda Ngozi Adichie', *Esquire*, 29 April 2019 (accessed 26 November 2023) https://www.esquire.com/uk/culture/a27283913/still-becoming-at-home-in-lagos-with-chimamanda-ngozi-adichie/.

11 Maryam Kazeem, 'Eyimofe (This Is My Desire): Floating Currencies', *The Criterion Collection*, 26 April 2022 (accessed 20 June 2024) https://www.criterion.com/current/posts/7756-eyimofe-this-is-my-desire-floating-currencies.

12 *Raindrops*, directed by Stephen Okoth Ochieng (Based on a true story. Produced by Stephen Okoth 2019, 3 min.), Kenyan filmmaker-photographer Stephen Okoth was a finalist in the micro-fiction category of the We Art Water Film Festival 5, 2019/2020 (accessed 2 June 2024) https://www.wearewater.org/en/kibera-the-slum-as-a-symptom_340571 https://www.wearewater.org/en/we-art-water-film-festival-5-an-in-depth-journey-through-the-value-of-water_338711.

13 Kounkuey Design Initiative, Kibera Public Space Project, Prize for Cities 2020-2021 (accessed 20 October 2023) https://www.youtube.com/watch?v=ujpcvgxXYRI. See also: WRI Ross Center Prize for Cities, 2020-2021 Finalist, Kibera Public Space Project, (accessed 24 May 2024) https://prizeforcities.org/project/kibera-public-space-project. See also: Etta Madete, 'Gardens of Kibera: The Kibera Public Space Project by Kounkuey Design Initiative', *Architectural Review*, 8 February 2021, Kibera Public Space Projects in Nairobi by Kounkuey Design Initiative deliver open spaces and sanitation with the community to combat deprivation and overcrowding (accessed 20 October 2023) https://www.architectural-review.com/buildings/gardens-of-kibera-the-kibera-public-space-project-by-kounkey-design-initiative.

14 UNESCO Field Office Nairobi (accessed 20 October 2023) https://www.unesco.org/fr/fieldoffice/nairobi/about.

15 Goethe Institute, Toronto, Canada Film Screening, 'One Fine Day – Africa Now', 5–12 March 2019, presented by the Goethe-Institut, co-presented with the Toronto Black Film Festival (accessed 11 October 2023) https://www.goethe.de/ins/ca/en/sta/tor/ver.cfm?fuseaction=events.detail&event_id=21445406. See also: James Hodapp, excerpt in Project Muse from his review, 'Nairobi Half Life by David Gritonga', *African Studies Review* 57 no. 1 (2014): pp. 231–233. *Project MUSE*, https://muse.jhu.edu/article/543448/pdf.

16 AbdouMaliq Simone, 'Black Urbanism, Life at the Extensions', lecture at the School of Materialist Research, 18 August 2022 (accessed 15 October 2023). https://www.youtube.com/watch?v=ReZOZuZv0Ns.

17 David Dodman, et al., 'African Urbanisation and Urbanism: Implications for Risk Accumulation and Reduction', *International Journal of Disaster Risk Reduction* 26 (2017): pp 7–15, ISSN 2212-4209 (accessed 20 November 2022) https://doi.org/10.1016/j.ijdrr.2017.06.029. See also, https://www.sciencedirect.com/science/article/pii/S2212420917300237 On page 8, section 1.1.2, the authors explain the typical improvised formation of informal settlements in cities: 'urban sprawl comes with significant costs. For those who cannot afford cars or even formal public transport, the need to live within cycling or walking distance of employment hubs may mean that people find or build homes in hazardous areas within and around the city, such as floodplains, mangrove swamps and unstable hillsides, where formal development has been prohibited'.

Chapter 4

HYBRIDITIES

The films selected for this chapter manifest contemporary hybridities in Africa: Chinese, European, Soviet, North and South American influences; cultural critiques and theoretical influences; infrastructural and urban influences such as the interventions during the Soviet era, and now by China. The impact of Chinese investment on African infrastructure and, by extension, on social daily spaces and landscapes has been far-reaching, and it is the African continent's largest trading and debt partner. Examples of controversial repayment issues are rife, and China's threat to take over Entebbe International Airport in Uganda, for non-payment of a loan secured in 2015 from China's Exim Bank made headline news in mainstream newspapers such as *Le Monde*.[1] Another news item in *Le Monde* in 2018 reported that the headquarters of the African Union in Addis Ababa, whose building was constructed by the Chinese in 2012, had discovered that its IT system, also set up by the Chinese, had hidden espionage equipment that had been secretly transferring all the union's data to Shanghai.[2] However the effects of the pandemic on the economy slowed the pace of Chinese investment activity.

Yuhi Amuli, *A Taste of Our Land*, Rwanda/Uganda, 2020, 70 Minutes

Set in a nameless African country, land ownership is the pivotal issue in this drama. Based on the director's own experiences working in a Chinese-run mine in Rwanda, the film underscores greed, corruption, land-grabbing and the continued exploitation of Indigenous people and workers by foreign mining companies.

The film opens with a quote from the novel *Petals of Blood* by Ngũgĩ Wa Thiong'o:

This land used to yield. Rains used to not fail. What happened? inquired Ruoro.

It was Muturi who answered. 'You forget that in those days the land was not for buying. It was for use. It was also plenty, you need not have beaten one yard over and over again'.[3]

Panoramic views of luxuriant rural forested landscapes, typical of the film's location, predominate in this drama and contrast firmly with shots of a desolate terrain ravaged by the indurate exploitation of land by a foreign mining company that has also created social havoc in the community.

The story is centred on Yohani (Michael Wawuyo), a local landowner who is attempting to sue the Chinese owners of a mine that is destroying his land. In the eight years of the mine's existence, he has received no compensation from the government and is now demanding 50 per cent of the takings from the mine owners.

As lanky Yohani rides his rickety bicycle towards the mine, he passes by the rugged natural beauty of the hillsides, river, and mountainous landscape, and the film's locations present the appeal of traditional town elements: winding streets, meadows, local housing, church and prison. His anxieties about finance and his wife's difficult pregnancy have made it even more urgent to resolve his property claim. While struggling to communicate his demands for compensation with the Chinese convict-manager Cheng (Peter Kye), Yohani cannot contain his frustration and complains bitterly about the desecration of his ancestral land and its decrepit condition. But in an early narrative twist, when Yohani suddenly discovers a gold nugget on the site, he sees his fortune changing and will do anything to hold on to it. The plot swerves to follow nugget's ricocheting trail from the depths of a sewer to the hands of those coveting the gold to inside of Yohani's stomach as he languishes in jail.

The director's concerns include the need to raise awareness of the abuse of citizens' rights by foreign companies operating in African countries. The main narrative illustrates some of the transgressions of foreign mining companies in exploiting both the resources and the local population in the detailed dialogues between the mine overseer Cheng with Yohani and then with Gangi (Michael Sseguija), a mine employee. Before joining Yohani in the quest to find a buyer for the gold nugget, Gangi tries to get a formal job description and contract, stopping at the overseer's office. This list of employment demands may evoke the basic exploitation that the director experienced in his work in a Rwandan mine. In the discussion with Cheng, the overseer hands him a single-page document written in Chinese. When Gangi asks for an English or French copy, Cheng replies sarcastically, 'Why not learn Chinese? What do you expect from a Chinese company?' When Gangi asks for a job description, the reply is simple: 'There is no such thing. Just do what I tell you to do'.

Gangi persists and asks, 'What does it say about my rights as an employee? What about my medical insurance?' But Cheng scoffs and says, 'You can sign or work underground'.

The futile exchange drags on as Cheng states that just a contract is a favour. Gangi signs, and asks for a copy. Exasperated, Cheng sighs and ignores him.

The characters in the plot can be seen as symbolically representing a variety of agents that have strongly impacted the African continent: the English surveyor-geologist with his pith helmet, a weakened former colonist, is easily overcome by the new Chinese influence in Africa, represented by Cheng, the rather caricatural depraved and cynical mine overseer character. The cartoonish, greedy and hypocritical priest plays his part representing the church in broad strokes as he grasps the gold nugget and also represents the corrupt, while the local police force symbolizes the good. The stalwart forces of the local police save Yohani and his group of friends from themselves as an officer views the CCTV camera footage that proves the perpetrator was Cheng.

The film's camerawork pans across the landscape: mountains, grassy pastures, the modest village and territory, and the rivers traversing the terrain. The visuals of the landscape convey a context and an underlying narrative that are, at least, as persuasive as the twisting plot. In the end, although justice is served, the story that cannot deliver a happy ending, nevertheless works to raise environmental and political awareness and to underscore the need for ethical and responsible development of the riches of the land.

Suzannah Mirghani, *Al-Sit*, 2021, Sudan/Qatar, 20 Minutes

Relying on both experienced and first-time local actors, the drama *Al-Sit* observes the precarious, waning power of the traditional matriarchal hierarchy, invested in the grandmother. The title *Al-Sit* is imbued with multiple meanings that can be translated as 'mistress of house'. The film was shot on location in a cotton farming area in the village of Aezzazh (also referred to as Azaza) and in Khartoum, and the narrative is structured around the traditional Sudanese practice of arranged marriage. Fifteen-year-old Nafisa (Mihad Murtada) is attracted to Babiker, a boy her age in the village, while her parents are arranging her marriage to Nadir (Mohammed Magdi), a young businessman who wants to bring in new machines to harvest cotton and make a profit at the expense of local customs. Al-Sit, played convincingly by Rabeha Mohammed Mahmoud (a respected Sudanese stage actor), has her own ideas about her granddaughter's future and reacts to the westernized suitor with a barbed comment on his shiny polyester suit before reeling off her extensive knowledge of his family network. As Nadir is being driven through cotton fields to the village to meet his prospective parents-in-law, the driver laughs and says, 'God will help you with Al-Sit'.

Al-Sit's absolute confidence, her matriarchal status and authority stem in part from widowhood, giving her independence and ownership of cotton fields. She confides her plan to Nafisa and recommends that she marry an older man, so that she too would eventually be an independent widow and a companion for her grandmother.

Although Sudan remains very much a patriarchal society, the director emphasizes the significance of the ancient Sudanese tradition of matriarchal power, 'controlling the fate of women and girls in the household, especially when it comes to questions of marriage. Because of the matriarch's deep knowledge about the history and lineage of the extended family, she is also very often the matchmaker, and family members come to her for advice'.[4] As someone who did not experience an arranged marriage, Mirghani asks herself how a young girl, whose marriage is to be arranged, reacts to the decisions made by her grandmother. In an interview, Mirghani wonders about the contradictions of traditional matriarchy:

> I am always curious about what goes through the mind of a young girl when her life path is chosen by others in her family, and I have so many unanswered questions: How does this young girl feel about the situation? What does she truly desire?
>
> How is it that a young girl has no say whatsoever and yet another female, her grandmother, is the final decision-maker? How does one go from being utterly voiceless and vulnerable as a young girl to gaining so much power and prestige within her lifetime to become a matriarch?[5]

For Mirghani, young Nafisa, who does not utter a word in the film, a gesture can symbolize change in a 'small empowering moment for a girl who has no way out'.[6] However, the director has drawn on her family history and alludes to her grandparents' love story by naming the two teenagers, Nafisa and Babiker, after them.[7]

Mirghani is clear about the messages her short film carries, stating: 'I portray multiple Sudanese socio-political issues in this film, among them: arranged marriages, child marriages, filial piety, stubborn traditionalism, economic exploitation, women's rights, and power struggles between family members as well as between genders'.[8]

Teboho Edkins, *Days of Cannibalism: Of Pioneers, Cows and Capital*, Lesotho/France/South Africa/Netherlands. 2020, 78 Minutes

Set in Thaba-Tseka, Lesotho, a landlocked or enclave nation in the heart of South Africa, *Days of Cannibalism* is a hybrid reality-fiction film and could be characterized as a revisionist western. Filmed in cinemascope like a western, the director has deliberately used the cinematic tropes of the western frontier, such as the race on horseback, to suggest the pioneering dynamics and the incongruities of Chinese merchant migrants arriving in Lesotho's mountainous landscape and confronting the peculiarities of Basotho culture, where cattle are both a spiritual symbol and a commodity, prime vessel for investment. (See Figure 4.1.)

In an interview for the Film Festival Köln 2021, Teboho Edkins interprets the visual impact of the unfenced, open landscape in Lesotho as a collective utopian political concept. As a result of the country's history, land is not easily available for purchase by foreigners, unlike its neighbouring countries such as South Africa and Namibia, where great tracts of territory are fenced off and privately owned, much of it by local white farmers or foreigners. He notes that, typically, it is the male partner of a Chinese immigrant couple who will obtain Lesotho citizenship in order to purchase property. He speculates on the visual effect of the open landscape, perhaps conveying the idea of a communist or socialist landscape.[9]

In another interview at the 70th Berlin Film Festival in 2020, Edkins talks of the high crime rate in Lesotho and, giving an example of what he calls 'directed reality', he describes an actual incident when he, his crew of two and his Chinese companions were leaving a Chinese store when they were attacked, tied up, beaten and robbed. Since the crew's camera was stolen, the director incorporated the shop's CCTV footage into the documentary. Conversely, in a fictional reality episode, when portraying the trial, the director recreated a courtroom scene following the real trial of cattle rustlers, who were given a severe 10-year prison sentence for theft and for selling the animals that ultimately were butchered. Filming in the courtroom was not permitted during the actual trial, but the same convicted rustlers, the trial judge and the prosecutor, playing themselves and unscripted, re-enacted the trial process over several hours in the same location, the same courtroom and followed the same proceedings, including a scene in which the two Basotho cattle thieves and former miners explain that their motives for stealing cattle, which they sold to Chinese businessmen to be slaughtered, were a consequence of unemployment in Lesotho in the mining industry.[10]

The director discusses the mythical and spiritual role of cattle in Basotho society, a phenomenon which, in a critique on the failed Thaba-Tseka Development Project in Lesotho between 1975 and 1984, the anthropologist James Ferguson identified 'herd hoarding' as a response to the migration of Basotho males to work in South African mines. Explaining this in his review of the film, Giorgio Blundo adds that the arrival of Chinese merchants is not recent, but dates back to the 1960s.[11] Teboho Edkins also mentions that the

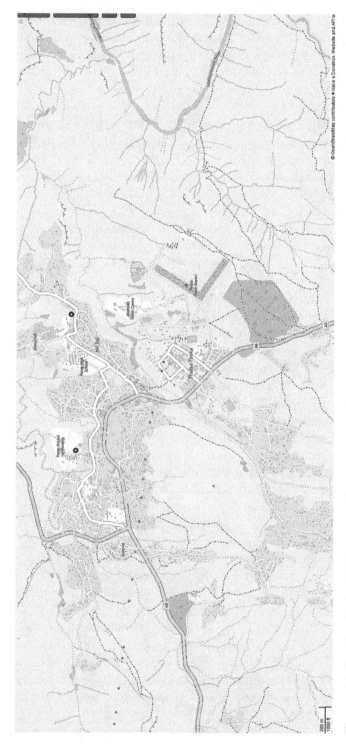

Figure 4.1 Lesotho, Thaba-Tseka, courtesy Open Street Map. (Film referenced: *Days of Capitalism: of Pioneers, Cows and Capital.*)

first wave of far eastern immigrants to Lesotho were Taiwanese, followed by the Chinese from Beijing and recently from the Fujian region.[12]

Edkins directed a 27-minute short documentary film on a related topic, entitled *Shepherd*, which is also set in Lesotho and examines the 'bovine mystique' (James Ferguson, 1994) in a prison context. A prisoner demonstrates his profound regret, which is expressed in dreams of his cow and sometimes sheep. Most offenders are penalized a year for each theft of a cow.

Even though their documentary approaches are entirely different, there is a coincidental correspondence between the documentary *Buddha in Africa* set in Malawi, by South African director Nicole Schrader, and Edkins' *Orphanage* (2020), a short film about a Buddhist orphanage in Lesotho: the Amitofo Care Center organization, established in Likupa, in western Lesotho, in 2008.

Nicole Schafer, *Buddha in Africa*, South Africa, 2020, 90 Minutes

The documentary, *Buddha in Africa*, critiques the effects of so-called soft power through the cultural interventions of a Chinese Buddhist orphanage in Malawi. The Amitofo Care Center (ACC) is located in Blantyre (a city with a population of approximately one million inhabitants) and was founded in 2004 by Hui-li, a Buddhist monk from Taiwan, in response to the AIDS epidemic. When Schafer was living in Malawi, the numerous orphanages there caught her attention, which she recalls in an interview with the magazine *Variety*: (See Figure 4.2.)

> I was working on a story for Reuters' magazine program *Africa Journal* about orphans in Malawi at a time that Madonna was adopting her second child [from Malawi] Mercy James in 2009. I was actually quite surprised during this period of research that there were quite a number of different orphanages or institutions promoting different cultural practices, from the Dutch Reformed Christian institutions to Islamic Turkish ones. Madonna subsequently set up her Kabbalist institution too.[13]

In the introduction to her film, the director outlines her critique of this institutional approach:

> I was struck by how this orphanage was strangely reminiscent of the Christian missions during the colonial era – only here African children had Chinese names and instead of learning about the West, they were learning about Chinese culture and history. I felt the orphanage would be the perfect metaphor to explore the growing relationship between China and Africa, but also as a mirror of Western colonialism.[14]

Figure 4.2 Malawi, Blantyre, courtesy Open Street Map. (Film referenced: *Buddha in Africa.*)

The camera documents daily life at the ACC and follows the main character, Enock Alu Bello, who was given the Chinese name Alu and was one of the first children to be housed at the centre. He arrived at age six or seven to train and rapidly excelled in the Chinese martial art Shaolin kung fu, which is central to Han Buddhism education, and which the ACC also uses as a fundraising tool. The director follows Enock's education and his participation as the child star in demonstrations by a martial arts team in front of cheering audiences who hailed him and singled him out by name, shouting 'Alu', at many fundraising events held in Taiwan, Hong Kong, China, Singapore, Malaysia, Thailand, Japan, Cambodia, New Zealand, Australia and the United States.

Enock yearns for daily life in his village, where he had lived with his extended, mostly female family, his grandmother and aunts, after his mother died and his father had abandoned him to start another family, leaving him a virtual orphan. His father died when Enock was four. According to the writer and musician Masauko Chipembere in a review of Schafer's film, Enock comes originally from Mangochi, several hundred kilometres north of the mountainous Chiradzulu district, south of Lake Malawi, which at the turn of the century was home to the revolutionary Baptist pastor Reverend John Nkologo Chilembwe. Mangochi is mostly inhabited by the Yao (or WaYao) people, who are 'predominantly Muslim and their language is known as Chi-Yao', which, as he grew up, Enoch forgot how to speak, as he was surrounded by people who speak Chi-Chewa, Malawi's principal language spoken by the Christian majority.[15] Chipembere also notes several important contextual issues in Mangochi, such as the local socio-economic conditions arising from unemployment and the departure of adult males to find work in South African mines, which resulted in 'families that were left fatherless by the constant migration of able-bodied men' and villages without adult males.[16]

When Enock is offered the opportunity to continue his studies in Taiwan, he is filmed visiting with his grandmother in his former village. He looks downcast and seems troubled. After some hesitation, he expresses his wish to live in the village with his grandmother and not accept the study programme. But his family explains to him that his grandmother will soon be too elderly to care for him, and they hope to depend on him. He returns to the ACC to accept the offer of education in Taiwan.

The exhilarating martial arts training and performance are an entertaining aspect of the film. However, Xiao Bei, the martial arts trainer, reveals the underlying cruelty of his discipline, as well as the lack of a bond with the young teenage students. This leads to one of the documentary's most dramatic moments of confrontation, when students disobey him, and when he threatens them, they retaliate and overpower him.[17]

The ACC Amitofo Care Center, a Buddhist organization founded in 2004, is an international charity registered in the US. First operating in Blantyre, Malawi, it expanded to Lesotho in 2008 (with a second site in 2014), Eswatini (Swaziland) in 2011, Mozambique in 2012, Namibia in 2015, a second centre in Lilongwe, Malawi (2016) and Moramanga in Madagascar (2019).[18]

Notes

1 Elias Biryabarema, 'China Rejects Allegations it may Grab Ugandan Airport if Country Defaults on Loan', *Reuters*, 29 November 2021 (accessed 12 December 2023) https://www.reuters.com/markets/rates-bonds/china-rejects-allegations-it-may -grab-ugandan-airport-if-country-defaults-loan-2021-11-29/.

2 Ghalia Kadiri and Joan Tilouine, 'A Addis-Abeba, le siège de l'Union africaine espio-nné par Pékin', *Le Monde*, 26 January 2018 (accessed 11 December 2023) https://www .lemonde.fr/afrique/article/2018/01/26/a-addis-abeba-le-siege-de-l-union-africaine -espionne-par-les-chinois_5247521_3212.html. *'Il y a un an, les informaticiens du bâti-ment, construit en 2012 par les Chinois, ont découvert que l'intégralité du contenu de ses serveurs était transférée à Shanghaï.'* (A year ago, computer technicians working on the Chinese-built building completed in 2012, discovered the entire server content was transferred to Shanghai.) (author's translation) See also: 'China Dismisses "Absurd" African Union HA Spying Claim', *BBC*, 29 January 2018, https://www.bbc.com/news/world-africa -42861276.

3 Ngũgĩ Wa Thiong'o (pseudonym for James Ngugi), *Petals of Blood*. London: Heinemann, African series, 1st edition, 1977, p 82. See also: Yuhi Amuli, writer and director, interviewed by filmmaker and writer Timothy Niwamanya, *Cinema Red Pill* (podcast) #115, 14 March 2024 (accessed 25 May 2024) https://www.youtube.com/ watch?v=AacQnaOmcAo. Yuhi Amuli worked with Ugandan filmmakers for his film *A Taste of Our Land* and discusses the challenges of working in the local film industry in Rwanda and mentions that there are only three cinemas in Rwanda, which are all in the capital, Kigali.

4 John Higgins, 'Interview Special: Suzannah Mirghani: *Al-Sit*', *Film and TV Now*, 9 November 2021 (accessed 10 December 2023) https://www.filmandtvnow.com/ interview-special-suzannah-mirghani-al-sit/.

5 Suzannah Mirghani 'Interview with Suzannah Mirghani, director of Al-sit', inter-viewed by Abla Kandalaft, myDylarama, 2 July 2021 (accessed 10 December 2023) https://mydylarama.org.uk/Interview-with-Suzannah-Mirghani-director-of-Al-sit.

6 Q&A with filmmakers Elpida Stathatou, *Umbilical*; Suzannah-Mirghani, *Al Sit* and Pom Bunsermvicha, *Lemongrass Girl* from the Rituals programme at Encounters Film Festival 2021 (12 min.), hosted by Ren Scateni (accessed 10 December 2023) https:// www.encounters.film/alsit.

7 Suzannah Mirghani interviewed by Erfan Rashid, '*My Interviews*', 2020 (at 4 min.) (accessed 10 December 2023) https://womensliteracysudan.blog/2021/12/13/al-sit/.

8 Suzannah Mirghani, 'Behind Award-Winning Film *Al-Sit* and Filmmaker Suzannah Mirghani', interview by Ola Diab, *500words Magazine*, 15 April 2021 (accessed 22 May 2024) https://500wordsmag.com/interviews/behind-award-winning-film-al-sit -and-filmmaker-suzannah-mirghani/.

9 Christian Gallichio, 'Berlin Review: *Days of Cannibalism* a Harrowing, Profound Look at the Culture Wars in Lesotho', *The Film Stage*, 3 March 2020 (accessed 12 August 2023) https://thefilmstage.com/berlin-review-days-of-cannibalism-is-a-harrowing-profound-look-at-the-culture-wars-in-lesotho/.

10 Teboho Edkins, 'Teboho Edkins about *Days of Cannibalism*', interview by Lise Mercier, 15 September 2022, 18th edition of the Africa Film Festival in Cologne, (accessed 12 August 2023) https://vimeo.com/639461221.

11 Giorgio Blundo, 'Edkins Teboho, director. *Days of Cannibalism: Of Pioneers, Cows and Capital*', 2020. 78 min. Sesotho, Fujianese, Mandarin, English, with English and French subtitles. China and Lesotho. Produced by KinoElektron, Day Zero Films, Kepler Film.' review, *African Studies Review* 66, no. 1 (1 March 2023): 288–290, published online, Cambridge University Press, (5 September 2022) https://doi.org/10.1017/asr.2022.120. Published by HAL Id: hal-03963218 30 January 2023 (accessed 10 October 2023) https://hal.science/hal-03963218 Blundo refers to the anthropologist James Ferguson and his work, *The Anti-Politics Machine. Development, Depoliticization, and Bureaucratic Power in Lesotho* (The University of Minnesota Press, 1994):

> 'But Ferguson showed that there was nothing traditional about these practices. Rather, they were the result of the migration of Basotho men to the mining areas of South Africa. Herd hoarding, far from being the classic example of contemplative herding popularized by anthropological literature, has long been a means of supporting the extended family back in Lesotho and of securing one's own retirement at the same time. Teboho thus captures longstanding social and economic changes; the economy of Thaba-Tseka has long been more dependent on wage labour in South African mines and factories than on agriculture and livestock. Similarly, the Chinese presence in Lesotho is not recent but dates to the 1960s.

12 Teboho Edkins, 'Q & A *Days of Cannibalism* with Teboho Edkins', interviewed by La Frances Hui, curator at MOMA, New directors New films, 2020, presented by Film at Lincoln Centre and MOMA, 1 January 2021 (accessed 10 December 2023) https://www.youtube.com/watch?v=obpAjaELqZ4.

13 Christopher Vourlias, '*Buddha in Africa* Director Nicole Schafer on China's Soft Power Play', *Variety*, 19 November 2019 (accessed 15 November 2023) https://variety.com/2019/film/festivals/idfa-buddha-in-africa-nicole-schafer-1203198833/. See also: Kamiyala Kondwani, 'Film on Malawian Boy Going World Places', *Nation Online*, 20 September 2019 (accessed 18 June 2023) https://mwnation.com/film-on-malawian-boy-going-world-places/.

14 Chanelle Ellaya, '*Buddha in Africa* provides a unique perspective on Chinese soft power in Africa', *Screen Africa*, 4 October 2019 (accessed 15 November 2023) https://www.screenafrica.com/2019/10/04/film/film-content/buddha-in-africa-provides-a-unique-perspective-on-chinese-soft-power-in-africa/. See also: Chanelle Ellaya, writer and manager and project coordinator at Ladima foundation, articles on *Muck Rack* (accessed 23 May 2024) https://muckrack.com/chanelle-ellaya/articles.

15 Masauko Chipembere, writer and musician 'Buddha in Africa', *Africa is a Country*, 2 July 2020 (accessed 18 June 2023) https://africasacountry.com/2020/07/buddha-in-africa.

16 Ibid.

17 Heng Yeh Yee, Buddha in Africa: An Imbalance of Power? Handful of leaves.life, (website) 22 September 2023 (accessed 20 June 2024) https://handfulofleaves.life/buddha-in-africa-when-does-dhamma-propagation-go-too-far/. According to Heng Yeh Yee, the ACC coach Xiao Bei was charged with assault and deported. See also: Xuefei Shi and Hangwei Li, 'Chinese Buddhism in Africa: The Entanglement of Religion, Politics and Diaspora', *Contemporary Buddhism* 23, no. 1–2 (August 2023): pp. 1–23 (accessed 15 June 2024) DOI:10.1080/14639947.2023.2242074; https://www.researchgate.net/publication/373506253_Chinese_Buddhism_in_Africa_The_Entanglement_of_Religion_Politics_and_Diaspora.

18 Dr. Yang Ganfu, Correspondent, 'Opinion - Amitofo Care Centre and Buddhism in Africa (Part 2)', *New Era*, 7 November 2023 (accessed 12 December 2023) https://neweralive.na/posts/opinion-amitofo-care-centre-and-buddhism-in-africa-part-2.

Chapter 5

FUTURITIES

The films in this chapter address themes of futurities, digital technologies of the moving image, socio-cultural movements and cultural restitution. In an interview with the journalist Oulimata Gueye, the Kenyan writer and film director Wanuri Kahiu debates science fiction and whether the layered contemporary meanings and interpretations of Afrofuturism are a trend. Kahiu said she considers science fiction to be a longstanding feature of the African oral tradition, stating there have always been

> people in all parts of Africa that have either looked to space, or [...] who are seers, who could see into the future, and who could disseminate the future and tell people what is going to happen, so we've always been able to draw from things that are outside of this world to be able to make sense of what is inside of the world.[1]

Wanuri Kahiu, *Pumzi*, Kenya, 2009, 20 Minutes

In the short film *Pumzi* (meaning breath in Swahili), the Nairobi-based director imagines a future dystopian world and inadvertently ventures via science fiction into the lively genre of Afrofuturism. In the scenario, survivors of a World War Three, the 'Water War', live in a hermetic underground society. This future is a totalitarian, technocratic culture governed by military personnel. The protagonist, Asha (Kudzani Moswela), like all citizens, must wear tubes to recycle her bodily fluids in a context of extreme water scarcity and chooses to break free to the contaminated surface.[2]

Asha, a scientifically trained conservator, works alone in an almost empty laboratory of a sanitized natural history museum. She is a member of a hierarchical and fully technocratic society, lodged far underground after a water war contaminated the surface. Water is so scarce in this quiet chthonian environment that she and her co-inhabitants use grafted-on tubing to recycle their bodily fluids through frequent exercise. When Asha receives an anonymous, unauthorized parcel containing a jar of soil with high humidity content and no radioactivity, she contacts her superior who appears remotely on a screen without uttering words. Communication is transmitted and monitored by an unknown process. Her superior does not believe Asha. She orders her to throw the sample away and to take her dream suppressant medication. Asha breaks the rules and plants a seed in the soil, waters it and observes it grow. Three senior administrators, stern, menacing women in dark military uniform, who possibly represent a matriarchal power structure, appear on her screen to harshly reprimand her. As punishment, they send in a tactical security squad of uniformed men who burst in, smash the museum display cases and drag Asha away to the exercise equipment room, where she is ordered to exercise until she has filled a bottle with her excess bodily fluids. When she goes to the toilets, the cleaner (Chantelle Burger), who had surreptitiously removed the live plant in its container from the museum, now places it discreetly on the sink counter. Asha secures it in her clothing and makes a break for the outside world on the surface.

On earth's dangerously contaminated surface, Asha fashions protective clothing, sandals and headscarf from among the debris and discarded textiles, waste being spouted from a culvert. She wanders and explores through an arid desert landscape, searching for a place she has dreamt of where she can plant the seedling and for which she is prepared to pay the ultimate sacrifice.

Wanuri Kahiu, *Rafiki*, Kenya, 2018, 83 Minutes

The fiction feature film *Rafiki*, meaning friend in Kiswahili, and set in Nairobi, Kenya, was inspired by *Jambula Tree*, a short story, which won the £10,000 Caine Prize for African Writing in 2007, by the Ugandan writer Monica Arac de Nyeko and which is also the title piece of a collection of short stories by other shortlisted authors. Written in letter form, the story is set in the Nakawa-Naguri housing estate, the largest public housing project in Kampala, Uganda, and relates the love between two young women, who are separated when their affair becomes known.[3] The narrative features two full-figured young girls, Anyango and Sanyu, who grow up together and become intimate in adolescence, then are caught under the Jambula tree. Sanyu is sent away, and five years later, Anyango sends a letter from Kampala to London, where Sanyu has been exiled, at the time of a rumour of her impending return. As is well known, many African countries criminalize homosexuality, and penalization is particularly severe in Uganda, notorious for its legislation punishing homosexual relations.[4] (See Figure 5.1.)

Wanuri Kahiu adapted the original story by Arac de Nyeko. Kahiu's adaptation, co-written with South African filmmaker Jenna Bass, expands on the story's plot and characterization but remains true to its main themes,

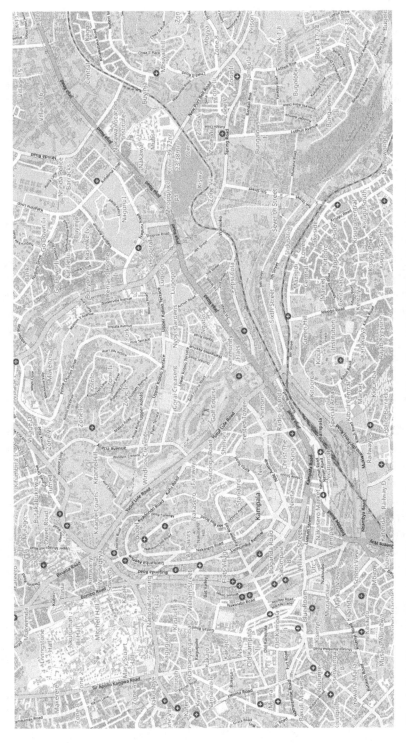

Figure 5.1 Uganda, Kampala, Nakawa housing estate, courtesy Open Street Map. (Film referenced: *Rafiki*.)

particularly the intervention of the local gossip, Mama Atim (Muthoni Gathecha), whose role as a judgemental commentator, as she broadcasts fresh neighbourhood rumours, drives the film's suspense and sometimes the action. The film script adds several sympathetic male characters to the story, which include Kena's father, John Mwaura (Jimmy Gathu), the shopkeeper of a small convenience store kiosk and her friend, Blacksta (Neville Misati).

Rafiki's story centres around the love between two teenage girls, Kena (Samantha Mugatsia) and Ziki (Sheila Munyiva), who meet and fall in love in a housing estate on the city outskirts with the fictional name of 'The Slopes' in Nairobi, Kenya. The script's new subplot is a political election for the County Assembly that involves both girls' fathers, Kena's father, John, representing the working classes, seeks to defeat Ziki's father, Peter Okemi (Dennis Musyoka), who runs a more upscale and better-financed campaign. When Mama Atim supervises her daughter Nduta (Nice Githinji) serving sodas to the two schoolgirls at her snack kiosk on their first outing together in public, she loses no time in playing on their fathers' rivalry and broadcasting their developing friendship as news to report.

Tomboyish Kena, an adroit football player, scoring goals in games with the guys, is also a responsible student and good citizen. She cares for her mother, Mercy (Nini Wacera), a religious zealot who is suffering from the end of her marriage. But Kena endures her mother's religious zeal, her narrow vision of love and her extremely hostile reaction to lesbian romance. Meanwhile, Kena's father, although happy in his recent remarriage and his young wife's pregnancy, shows concern for both his daughter and his ex-wife's reactions.

Ziki is exuberant and outgoing, with long, bubble-gum pink and blue hair extensions, and she first appears as the flamboyant centre of a trio of girls practising their coordinated dance moves posing on the outdoor staircase in the passageway of a housing complex. As the two girls' friendship blossoms into love, Mama Atim's ceaseless gossiping ignites a violent episode in which the girls are separated.

The film directly addresses the lack of gay rights in Kenya, which is underscored with the haunting character Tom (Vitalis Wawera), who is tacitly gay and systematically harassed whenever he encounters Kena's male crew. The film's narrative plays out in a boisterous, colourful setting, in a mixed middle- and lower-middle-class neighbourhood with glimpses of comfortable contemporary housing and urban living in Nairobi's arrays of both affordable and upmarket five- and six-storey apartment blocks, juxtaposed with lower-income housing in the lively neighbourhood set off with shots of hanging laundry, cluttered back stairs and animated street life.

Recently, Uganda announced even more new and severe penalties regarding homosexuality, while Kenya continues to repress LGBTQ people with severe policies regarding homosexuality. And although Kahiu espouses a light, playful 'AfroBubbleGum' spirit, she has addressed issues that directly affect the destinies and mental health of young people. *Rafiki* is banned in Kenya; however, the director succeeded in gaining permission to screen it for a week at the 2018 Cannes festival.[5]

Laurent Védrine, *Restituer l'art africain, les fantômes de la colonisation*, France, 2021, 62 Minutes

Some of the controversial and ongoing issues surrounding the colonial practices of cultural pillaging and the restitution of artworks are addressed in Laurent Védrine's documentary, *Restituer l'art africain, les fantômes de la colonisation* (2021), in which prominent theorists such as the writer and academic Felwine Sarr, art historian Bénédicte Savoy and the historian Gabin Djimassè are interviewed.[6] (See Figure 5.2.)

The film includes the participation of many experts in the field. The Senegalese academic Felwine Sarr and the art historian Bénédicte Savoy were commissioned by Emmanuel Macron to write the report, *Rapport sur la restitution du patrimoine culturel africain. Vers une nouvelle éthique relationnelle* (Restitution of African Cultural Heritage. Toward New Relational Ethics, 2018) which has given rise to numerous significant events, notably, *Museotopia, Réflexions sur l'avenir des musées en Afrique* (Museotopia, reflections on the future of museums in Africa), an international seminar organized by Bénédicte Savoy with

Figure 5.2 Bénin, Dahomey Palace, courtesy of Laurent Védrine. (Film referenced: *Restituer l'art africain, les fantômes de la colonization.*)

Felwine Sarr at the Collège de France on 11 June 2019, as well as a course of eight lectures spread over two months between February and April 2020, entitled *Présence africaine dans les musées d'Europe*, given by Bénédicte Savoy at the Collège de France; both events raised questions and marked an academic reconsideration of the role of the traditional museum.[7]

In Védrine's documentary, Felwine Sarr warns against and emphasizes the limits of misconstruing pillaged artefacts as mere objects:

> We have found papers, texts that theorize heritage and posit that when a people is vanquished, not only should their wealth be taken, but also their spiritual oeuvres to prevent their starting afresh. Thus cultural pillaging was a systematic undertaking (author's translation).[8]

Bénédicte Savoy makes the point that there is a very strong link between the idea of empire, the idea of territorial occupation and the idea of culture and museums.[9] And in his book *Brutalism*, Achille Mbembe writes that 'it is not only a question of restoring materials, styles, decorations, and functions. How will we restore the meaning?'[10]

The sculpture *Dieu Gou*, a figurative statue by Ekplékendo Akati, is dedicated to Gou, the animist god of iron, blacksmiths, the forge and war, who offers protection from the enemy in battle. It is a sculptural assemblage on a human scale, described by the Louvre as forged, laminated, hammered, nailed and riveted metal, and it is an assembled, rather than a carved or moulded work. Its flattened hat-like headpiece is a kind of altar for votive offerings.[11]

The Beninois historian Gabin Djimassè describes the *Dieu Gou* sculpture as part of the pantheon of Dahomey's animist religion, who intervenes as a god of war in all that pertains to manipulating metal, and said that of the 26 works promised by France to be returned to Benin, *Dieu Gou* was the principal work that they wanted returned.[12] France classed the sculpture as 'inalienable' property of the nation, despite issues regarding its provenance. It was described as being found on a beach in 1894, even though that is known to be false. (See Figure 5.3.)

Laurent Védrine's documentary is centred around the *Dieu Gou* sculpture. It is accurately covered and is a call for action. There is an aspect that could be mentioned here in the context of the influence of African art on Europe. Between the end of the nineteenth century and 1935, when the statue was exhibited at the Musée d'ethnographie du Trocadero in Paris, there was a Paris-based artistic shift in painting and modern sculpture, which in part can be attributed to the African artefacts exhibited there. In addition to creating his own work, the sculptor and metalworker Julio Gonzalez also fabricated sculptures for Picasso and they collaborated on a number of sculptures,

Figure 5.3 Dieu Gou, modern version of the statue by contemporary artist Simonet Biokou, Porto Novo, Bénin, courtesy of Laurent Védrine. (Film referenced: *Restituer l'art africain, les fantômes de la colonisation.*)

including Picasso's sculpture of 1928 dedicated to Apollinaire, which is one of the works that was influenced by the *Dieu Gou* sculpture. In 1918, Gonzalez had worked on the Renault assembly line, where he learnt autogenous welding, a method of fabrication that allows solid slender pieces to be attached without filler, a welding technique that characterized his own work and which would revise the notion of sculpture from its antecedents as being primarily carved out of stone and wood, shaped in clay or moulded in metal, to include its materiality as assembled and collaged iron and other metals, and this reverberated with an awareness and admiration of assembled and collaged metal sculptural pieces that are indebted to the fabrication techniques of the *Dieu Gou* statue.[13]

France is not the only nation with a significant collection of African sculpture. Along with the British Museum and the Ethnologisches Museum, Berlin, there is a network of European and British museums with collections from the Kingdom of Benin that communicate as participants in the Benin Dialogue Group, with the aim of reuniting the works in a museum in Benin: Weltmuseum, Vienna, Austria; Museum am Rothenbaum, Hamburg, Germany; Staatliche Kunstammlungen, Dresden, Germany; Museum für Völkerkunde, Dresden, Germany; GRASSI Museum für Völkerkunde zu Leipzig, Leipzig, Germany; Linden-Museum, Stuttgart, Germany; Nationaal Museum van Wereldculturen, Netherlands; Museum of Archaeology and

Anthropology, Cambridge, UK; Pitt Rivers Museum, Oxford, UK; National Museums Scotland, UK.

An earlier documentary by Laurent Védrine, *Obelisque de la discorde*, (The Obelisk of Axum Controversy, 2006), addresses the restitution of the looted seventeen-hundred-year-old Obelisk of Axum (82 feet, 160 tonne) to Ethiopia. One of 120 Obelisks in the ancient city of Axum, it was removed to Italy in 1937 and then returned in 2005. In 1985, Laurent Védrine's father, Hubert, who was President Francois Mitterrand's diplomatic advisor between 1981 and 1985, negotiated the return of Korean artefacts, an ancient book referred to as the *Oegyujanggak Uigwe* to Korea.[14]

Manthia Diawara, *Maison Tropicale*, Portugal, 2008, 58 Minutes

The film *Maison Tropicale* by Manthia Diawara explores the impact of mid-century modern architecture, and its entry into the art market as large-scale sculpture, in the work of mid-twentieth-century French designer Jean Prouvé.

The Malian director Diawara and the Mozambique-born Portuguese artist Ângela Ferreira tracked the trajectory of the architect's three porta-ble housing prototypes destined for tropical and arid climates: one erected in Niamey, Niger, and two inter-connected buildings in Brazzaville, the Republic of the Congo, in the late 1940s. Diawara and Ferreira inspected the sites of three of Prouvé's built prototype tropical houses after they had been removed. Deconstructed and relocated in 2000, the displaced structures have been reappraised as valuable sculptures and have sold for very high prices.[15]

Jean Prouvé developed a series of aluminium and steel prototypes with dis-tinct detailing to suit the climates of each location, which also included trial, but unbuilt prototypes for the *Maison de Cameroun* (1958–1964) and a Saharan house, *la Maison du désert* (1958). In 2000, the gallerist Éric Touchaleaume located all three of the built African prototypes that he bought. He brought a team to dismantle them, pack them in shipping containers and bring them back to France where they were restored, later exhibited and then sold to buy-ers in Paris, London and New York.

Now based in Lisbon, the installation artist and photographer Ângela Ferreira was born in Maputo, formerly Lourenço Marques, Mozambique, and was educated in South Africa. Manthia Diawara was born in Mali and is now professor of comparative literature and film, and director of the Institute of African-American Affairs at New York University. Both Ferreira's and Diawara's works explore the post-colonial narrative of shared cultural herit-age between Africa and the West.

Ferreira invited Diawara to join her in examining the former locations of the Prouvé houses in Niamey and the two conjoined houses in Brazzaville, accompanied by the curator and artist Jurgen Böck. They interviewed the people they encountered living at these sites, such as the Tuaregs, whose nomadic dwellings had been erected on the Niamey site – and which could be considered a vernacular form of demountable dwelling. While talking to the Tuareg occupants at the site, they discovered that one couple, Artonnor Ibriahine and her husband, had been a former housekeeper, caretaker and gardener, respectively, at the Prouvé house for 30 years, and they had stayed on, squatting on the site.

In Brazzaville, they met with another long-time occupant, Mireille Ngatsé, who had been a landlady as well as a resident. Diawara said that with these encounters and discussions that gave such a diverse local perspective, he had begun to feel a sense of renewal. Mireille Ngatsé gave a series of informative details about what it was like to live in the house: that it had multiple rooms, and that it had been airy, fresh, not at all overheated, and exceptionally comfortable in hot weather.[16]

Diawara has emphasized that the film does not address Prouvé's finished products since they were no longer in place. It focusses instead on the spaces left by the structures' removal, such as the concrete plinth in Niamey, and in Brazzaville, where the site has been quite thoroughly transformed by new additions. However, the discursive approach opened up interesting discussions with individuals who recalled the dwellings.

The value of Jean Prouvé's built prefabricated prototypes has increased dramatically in recent decades. Even his functionally designed chairs, which were once mass-produced and standard furniture in French university cafeterias, are sold for significant amounts (€14,000).[17] On a positive note, if ever there was a demand to replicate and reassemble numerous house prototypes, the *Maisons tropicales* were designed and fully intended for mass production. The Niamey and Brazzaville *Maisons tropicales* could be rebuilt in situ since the prototypes were designed to be replicated as multiples, by means of the well-preserved architectural plans and specifications.

Streaming Practices: Architecture and Urbanism Online

Along with the surge in global urbanization, streamed presentations of urbanists', architects' and landscape designers' work have increased. Certain curatorial programming, such as the *World Around* and its recent *Radical Repair* series, presents lengthy back-to-back designer presentations.[18] Several of the architects discussed have multiple branch offices, even though some may be temporary site-specific locales, with the designers shuttling back and forth between continents for the duration of a project.

The London-based British-Ghanaian architect Sir David Adjaye's many projects for, and perspectives on, African cities have been influential, particularly his urban proposals and vision for Accra, which he explains in many videos and on-screen interviews. In the design project for Marine Drive in Accra, Adjaye developed elements of an initiative undertaken during the socialist government era of President Kwame Nkrumah (1957–1966). The project was analysed by the architectural historian Łukasz Stanek, who identified issues complicating the historiographic analysis of urban landscape design in the post-colonial context.[19]

Important projects currently undertaken by the office of Adjaye Associates include the EDO Museum of West African Art, being constructed in Bénin City, Nigeria, which incorporates facilities and laboratories for archaeological excavations, and the National Cathedral of Ghana in Accra, a project that was put on hold in 2023. Several of Adjaye's commissions are no longer led by the architect in the wake of misconduct allegations by three former employees. Nevertheless, he has been an influential voice for contemporary architecture in the African, as well as the British and American contexts.[20]

Dot.ateliers, a sustainable three-storey art studio, gallery and yard complex with residency apartments, designed by the office of Adjaye Associates and completed in 2022 for the influential painter Amoako Boafo in Accra, Ghana, returns to the urban scale that brought the architect's work its initial acclaim.

The community- and environmentally friendly approach of the Berlin-based architect, Diébédo Francis Kéré, whose sustainable buildings in his birthplace of Gando, Burkina Faso, launched a global practice that is deemed to be one of the most prestigious architectural design practices of the 2020s. His work has received wide recognition, including some of the most distinguished awards in architecture, such as the Pritzker Prize in 2022. His numerous recorded lectures and videos explain his re-evaluation of traditional local building practices in Burkina Faso and his use of local materials such as compressed earth brick and compacted earth floors. In one of Kéré's streamed and online videos, the architect demonstrates how hands-on local community participation and use of local building practices, including compacted earth brick, have been incorporated into the design and construction process.[21]

The work of architect Mariam Issoufou, founder of Atelier Masōmī in Niamey, now Mariam Issoufou Architects based in Niamey, New York and Zurich, also relates to emerging and internationally-diffused architecture, and she emphasizes the key influences of sustainable, cultural and climatic specificity in her approach. Mariam Issoufou also discusses the importance of learning about African architecture in relation to its history in a lecture at Harvard University, an event in the Aga Khan Lecture Program.[22] The award-winning Hikma Community Complex, a secular and religious centre designed by Issoufou and the Boston-based architect Yasaman Esmaili, in Dandaji, Niger and completed in 2018, includes the design and construction of a new mosque and the conversion of the unused mosque into a library. The project uses CEB (compressed earth brick) for reasons of climate sensitivity and sustainability.

The work of heritage architect-urbanist May al-Ibrashy, founder and chair of the Athar Lina Initiative (the name translates to 'the monument is ours') in Cairo, addresses the needs of, and offers opportunities to, the local population, while assessing and preserving ancient architecture and infrastructure. In particular, the work involves reclassifying and distinguishing historic urban forms from informal structures and districts. It is an important undertaking in the face of heritage buildings in Cairo's ancient quarters being slated for demolition and replacement, according to recent journalists' reports, with little citizen involvement.[23]

Tosin Oshinowo is a Lagos-based Nigerian architect and curator of the second Sharjah Triennale in 2023, whose firm, cmDesign Atelier, recently designed low-cost emergency housing for Ngarannam, a village in northern Nigeria, whose occupants were displaced by the jihadist group Boko Haram. She has presented her work in the annual streamed conference *The World Around*, 2023. She also curated the second Sharjah Architecture Triennial, 'The Beauty of Impermanence: An Architecture of Adaptability', held from 11 November 2023 to 10 March 2024 in Sharjah City, United Arab Emirates.[24]

Nzinga Biegueng Mboup is a Senegalese-Cameroonian architect based in Dakar. Co-founder with Nicolas Rondet of the bioclimatic architectural practice Worofila, her work focusses on passive design and sustainable materials, particularly CEB, which involves training contractors and workers. In collaboration with the architect Carole Diop and in a project called Dakarmorphose, she has researched the architecture of the Lebu community in Dakar and underlines the significance of heritage and public spaces. She recently began a research programme at the Canadian Centre for Architecture in Montreal, where she has oriented her analysis to respond to key questions:[25]

What is the material heritage of our cities and what can we learn from it?
What type of Senegalese architectural identity(ies) define our city?

The two questions are indicative of the broad relevance of Worofila's research and practice interests: the attention to materiality dovetails with an emphasis both on local culture and ecosystems, and connects with the research at the scale of the city on modern and pre-modern precedents, pointing at issues of public space and how to foster an urban milieu responsive to climate.

Notes

1 Wanuri Kahiu, film writer, director, 'Africa and Science Fiction: Meeting with Wanuri Kahiu', interview by journalist Oulimata Gueye as part of the exhibition, 'Si ce monde vous déplaît', FRAC (Fonds régional d'art contemporain de Lorraine) Lorraine, Metz, France, 2013 (accessed 27 December 2023) https://www.youtube.com/watch?v=SWMtgD9O6PU. See also: Afrobubblegum (accessed 1 June 2024) https://www.afrobubblegum.com/. Tade Thompson, 'Please Stop Talking About the "Rise" of African Science Fiction', *Lithub*, 19 September 2018 (accessed 1 June 2024) https://lithub.com/please-stop-talking-about-the-rise-of-african-science-fiction/.

2 *Pumzi* directed by Wanuri Kahiu (Inspired Minority Pictures, 2009) Vimeo (accessed 12 December 2023) https://vimeo.com/46891859. See also Wanuri Kahiu in transcribed conversation with film and theatre director Shariffa Ali, *e-flux*, https://www.e-flux.com/video/334045/pumzi/.

3 Monica Arac de Nyeko, et al., *Jambula Tree and Other Stories*. Oxford: New Internationalist, 2008.

4 Reuters, 'Uganda Enacts harsh Anti-LGBTQ Law Including Death Penalty', *Reuters* (Reporting by *Reuters* reporters in East Africa; Additional reporting by Rachel Savage and Bhargav Acharya in Johannesburg, Foo Yun Chee in Brussels, Steve Holland in Washington; Written by George Obulutsa; Eds. Aaron Ross, Andrew Cawthorne and Giles Elgood). 30 May 2023 (accessed 12 December 2023) https://www.reuters.com/world/africa/ugandas-museveni-approves-anti-gay-law-parliament-speaker-says-2023-05-29/.

5 Wanuri Kahiu, 'Wanuri Kahiu: "Avec "Rafiki", j'ai voulu raconter une belle histoire d'amour africaine"', interviewed by Marion Doucet, *Le Monde Afrique*, 8 May 2018 (accessed 12 December 2023) https://www.lemonde.fr/afrique/article/2018/05/08/wanuri-kahiu-avec-rafiki-j-ai-voulu-raconter-une-belle-histoire-d-amour-africaine_5296145_3212.html. J'ai récemment participé à la création du collectif AfroBubbleGum. – I recently joined in the creation of the AfroBubbleGum Collective movement). Explore Africa: The AfroBubbleGum movement), https://www.youtube.com/watch?v=aSjtxJNUclY See also, Nita Bhalla, 'Kenyan Court Refuses to Lift ban on Acclaimed Lesbian Romance Film', *Reuters,* 29 April 2020 (accessed 27 December 2023) https://www.reuters.com/article/idUSKBN22B25Z/. Bhalla writes that the ban was lifted in September 2018 for seven days to allow the film to compete in the Oscars.

6 The film has prior titles: *Dieu Gou, le retour d'une statue,* (when it was shown in 2023 at the Festival Vues d'Afriques in Montreal, Canada) and *Restituer l'art africain - La statue du dieu Gou.* Laurent Védrine discussed his documentary in a radio interview (in French) in 2021: *'Dieu Gou, le retour d'une statue ou comment sortir d'un débat de spécialistes?* Laurent Védrine, interviewed by Siegfried Forster. RFI, 16 April 2021 (accessed 2 June 2024) https://www.rfi.fr/fr/culture/20210416-dieu-gou-le-retour-d-une-statue-ou-comment-sortir-d-un-d%C3%A9bat-de-sp%C3%A9cialistes.

7 Bénédicte Savoye and Felwine Sarr, *Rapport sur la restitution du patrimoine culturel africain. Vers une nouvelle éthique relationnelle.* 29 November 2018 (accessed 10 October 2023) https://www.vie-publique.fr/rapport/38563-la-restitution-du-patrimoine-culturel

-africain. See also: *Museotopia, Réflexions sur l'avenir des musées en Afrique* (Museotopia, Reflexions sur l'avenir des musees en Afrique), International Seminar, organized by Felwine Sarr, Bénédicte Savoye, Collège de France, Paris. 11 June 2019 (accessed 1 June 2024) https://www.college-de-france.fr/fr/agenda/colloque/museotopia-reflex-ions-sur-avenir-des-musees-en-afrique/introduction. See also: Bénédicte Savoye, *Présence africaine dans les musées d'Europe*, course of eight lectures, Collège de France, 14 February–10 April 2020 (accessed 1 June 2024) https://www.college-de-france.fr/fr/ agenda/cours/presence-africaine-dans-les-musees-europe.

8 Felwine Sarr, interviewed in Laurent Védrine, *Restituer l'art africain, les fantômes de la colonization*. France: Temps Noir, 2021 at 63 min. 'Il y a des textes que l'on a trouvés où les gens ont théorisé la captation patrimoniale en disant que lorsque vous vainquez un peuple, il faut non seulement lui prendre ses richesses, mais il faut lui prendre ses oeuvres spirituelles pour l'empêcher de se reconstruire. Donc ça a été une entreprise systématique de pillage culturel'.

9 Bénédicte Savoy, interviewed in Laurent Védrine, *Restituer l'art africain, les fantômes de la colonization* (at 14 min.) 'Il y a un lien très fort entre l'idée d'empire, l'idée d'occupation de territoire étranger, et l'idée de culture et de musée'.

10 Achille Mbembe, *Brutalism*. Trans. Stephen Corcoran. Durham, NC: Duke University Press, 2023. Originally published as *Brutalisme*. Paris: La Découverte, 2020, p. 218. 'Il ne s'agit donc pas de restituer des matériaux, des styles, des décors et des fonctions. Comment restituera-t-on le sens?' p. 218.

11 Aux Quatre Coins du Monde, Pavilion des Sessions, Louvre (accessed 31 December 2023) https://www.louvre.fr/decouvrir/le-palais/aux-quatre-coins-du-monde.

12 Gabin Bernard Djimassè in *Restituer l'art africain, les fantômes de la colonization* by Laurent Védrine (Facebook trailer 2021 at 3,45 min. He asserts, Dieu Gou was the work that they wanted returned) (accessed 10 October 2023) https://www.facebook .com/france5/videos/275835940694067/.

13 'Julio Gonzalez, Pablo Picasso and the Dematerializaton of Sculpture', Exhibition, curators Tomàs Llorens and Boye Llorens Peters, Fundacion MAPFRE, Madrid, 23 September 2022–8 January 2023 (accessed 1 June 2024) https://www.fundacion-mapfre.org/en/art-and-culture/exhibitions/historical/year-2022/gonzalez-picasso/. See also: Harry Bellet, 'Pablo Picasso et Julio Gonzalez en 170 œuvres exposées à Madrid: deux artistes pour une alliance de fer', *Le Monde*, 7 December 2022 (accessed 12 November 2023) https://www.lemonde.fr/culture/article/2022/12/07/pablo -picasso-et-julio-gonzalez-en-170-uvres-exposees-a-madrid-deux-artistes-pour-une -alliance-de-fer_6153301_3246.html. *Le Monde* English translation, Harry Bellet, 'A Madrid Exhibition Shows the Iron Pact Between Pablo Picasso and Julio Gonzalez', 13 December 2022 (accessed 1 June 2024) https://www.lemonde.fr/en/culture/arti-cle/2022/12/13/pablo-picasso-and-julio-gonzalez-in-170-works-exhibited-in-madrid -an-iron-pact-between-two-artists_6007558_30.html. Digital Benin, digital database (accessed 10 October 2023) https://digitalbenin.org/catalogue?seed=f2c60814-d106 -4b67-a41e-ee66f56a1fc0&page=1.

14 Hyun-kyung Kang, 'Return of Looted Artefacts Needs Careful Diplomacy', *Korea Times*, 29 November 2010 (accessed 15 October 2023) https://www.koreatimes.co.kr /www/nation/2023/06/113_77136.html. The article notes Laurent Védrine's family history. Presumably, Vedrine's expertise stems somewhat from his father Hubert's influ-ence. Hubert Védrine, closely involved in artefact restitution, was French foreign minis-ter and later presidential chief of staff under President Francois Mitterrand, 1997–2002.

15 Alastair Gordon, 'Out of Africa, a House Fit for a Kit Bag', *New York Times,* 1 July 2004 (accessed 5 August 2023) https://www.nytimes.com/2004/07/01/garden/out -of-africa-a-house-fit-for-a-kit-bag.html.

16 Mireille Ngatsé interviewee in *Maison Tropicale* (Maumaus, Portugal, 2008, at 23 min.) by Manthia Diawara, emphasizes the freshness and coolness of Prouvé's *Maison Tropicale* in Brazzaville, DRC.

17 Artcurial auctioneers, 31 May 2021 (accessed 10 October 2023) https://www.artcu-rial.com/fr/lot-jean-prouve-1901-1984-chaise-metropole-305-dite-standard-circa -1950-4089-38.

18 'In Focus: Radial Repair', *The World Around,* 28 September 2023 (accessed 15 December 2023) https://theworldaround.com/.

19 Łukasz Stanek. 'Tracing the Marine Drive, Accra', Canadian Centre for Architecture (accessed 15 October 2023) https://www.cca.qc.ca/en/articles/77853/tracing-the -marine-drive-accra. See also: David Adjaye Face to Face, interviewed by Godfred Akoto Boafo on the Cathedral and Marine Drive projects in Accra, Ghana, CITITV streamed on Facebook 18 September 2018 (accessed 2 June 2024) https://www.face-book.com/CitiTVGH/videos/face-to-face-with-david-adjaye-architect-designer-for -national-cathedral/526488801108011/.

20 Nour Fakharany, 'The Museum of West African Art Reveals Vision for a Vibrant Creative Hub in Benin City, Developed with Adjaye Associates', *ArchDaily,* 28 June 2023 (accessed 10 October 2023) https://www.archdaily.com/1003081/the-museum -of-west-african-art-reveals-vision-for-a-vibrant-creative-hub-in-benin-city-devel-oped-with-adjaye-associates. See also: David Adjaye in *Building Africa – Architecture of a Continent,* BBC, first shown, June 2005 director and producer John Holdsworth, British Broadcasting Corporation. London: BBC4, 2010 (accessed 1 June 2024) https://www.bbc.co.uk/programmes/b0074rfc and https://www.dailymotion.com/ video/xxlgcj.

21 A lecture by Diébédo Francis Kéré, architect, in 'Bridging the gap', Arc en rêve, con-ference, Centre d'architecture Bordeaux, 13 December 2012 (accessed 12 December 2023) (In French, at 43 min.) https://www.youtube.com/watch?v=TVlGMQqUpW4. Kéré emphasizes community participation and shows a team of local women working on clay floors in Burkina Faso. See also: Diébédo Francis Kéré, interviewed by Robin Merrill, *Insight Germany, DW News,* German public broadcasting. 5 June 2014 (accessed 27 December 2023) https://www.youtube.com/watch?v=JEYzonL9ecY&t=1s.

22 Mariam Issoufou Kamara, Aga Khan Program Lecture, Harvard Graduate School of Design, 7 March 2022 (accessed 10 October 2023) https://www.youtube.com/ watch?v=L9ZgkisSZkE. Mariam Issoufou discusses the importance of pre-colonial African history and the influence it had on her cultural education and criticizes inap-propriate of 'mimicry of western-style architecture' (at 7 min.). See also: https://www .gsd.harvard.edu/event/mariam-kamara/.

23 May al-Ibrashy, 'Athar Lina Initiative: Heritage as a Community Resource', lec-ture presented at the Architecture League, 5 June 2023 (accessed 11 November 2023) https://archleague.org/article/athar-lina-initiative-heritage-as-a-community -resource/. See also: Vivian Yee, 'A Modern Cairo, at History's Expense: Egypt's Government is Sacrificing Cultural Gems for Urban Renewal', *New York Times,* 27 August 2023, front page and page 10 (accessed 6 November 2023) https://static01 .nyt.com/images/2023/08/27/nytfrontpage/scan.pdf. and: another innovative bio-climatic restoration practice of historic settlements by an anthropologist architect in Morocco is found in the work of Salima Naji: https://salimanaji.com/.

24 Matthew Burgos, '"Rebuilding Ngarannam" in Nigeria Builds 500 Homes for Citizens Displaced by Boko Haram', *Designboom*, 10 July 2022 (accessed 6 November 2023) https://www.designboom.com/architecture/rebuilding-ngarannam-nigeria -tosin-oshninowo-07-10-2022/. See also: Nick Axel, 'Second Sharjah Architecture Triennial, The Beauty of Impermanence: An Architecture of Adaptability' Second Sharjah Triennial 11 November 2023–10 March 2024', *e-flux*, 8 December 2023 (accessed 27 December 2023) https://www.e-flux.com/criticism/579307/2nd -sharjah-architecture-triennial-the-beauty-of-impermanence-an-architecture-of -adaptability.

25 Nzinga Biegueng Mboup, architect and collaborator with CCA c/o Dakar to produce a series of public programs and research projects in Dakar, Senegal. 2023–2026, 1 July 2023 (accessed 6 November 2023) https://www.cca.qc.ca/en/cca-c-o/90157/ dakar. See also: Jori Lewis, 'The Future of Mud', *The Atlantic*, 5 July 2022 (accessed 22 June 2023) https://www.theatlantic.com/science/archive/2022/07/senegal-dakar -construction-mud-architecture/661405/. A Senegalese architecture firm is championing a lower-tech material than concrete to help cities prepare for climate change. Hana Abdel, 'Living in Dakar, A Study of Senegalese Housing & Future Development (by Nzinga Mboup and Caroline Geffriaud)', *ArchDaily*, 29 January 2021 (accessed 22 June 2023) https://www.archdaily.com/955865/living-in-dakar-a-study-of-senega -lese-housing-and-future-development. The Architectural and Urban development of Dakar, Excerpts from 'Dakarmorphose', a research project carried out by architects Carole Diop and Nzinga Mboup on Lébou villages and the urban and cultural heritage of the city of Dakar. Seleb-Yoon Gallery, December-March 2023 (accessed 22 June 2023) https://www.selebe-yoon.com/research-room/the-architectural-and -urban-development-of-dakar.

Chapter 6

SUSTAINABILITIES

This selection of films covers a range of issues that address the urgent need for sustainable, ecological urban and landscape strategies, taking into account biomes, ecosystems, biodiversity, reforestation and the ever-important question of water scarcity or excess (flooding). Contemporary documentary film is engaged in advancing the case for environmental justice, demonstrating the complex interaction of environmental requirements with economic development, the role of women and traditional social structures.

Aïssa Maïga, *Marcher sur l'eau (Above Water)*, France, 2021, 90 Minutes

Marcher sur l'eau is a full-length documentary that follows the seasons in the settlements of a formerly nomadic people obliged to settle near scarce and diminishing water sources, and demonstrates how providing water by drilling boreholes deep underground to reach the aquifer can impact their lives and help to mitigate the depredations of climate-change-induced desertification caused by drought, and eventually lead to the reintroduction of pastureland and vegetation in Niger.

The village of Tatiste is a settlement of semi-nomadic people in the Azawagh region, with Abalak as its nearest town and administrative centre. It is inhabited by the Fulani Wodaabi people, whose former traditional nomadic way of life is no longer feasible due to prolonged drought. The failure of several rainy seasons has obliged them to alter their roaming patterns. While the men leave on solo journeys to tend their herds, it is often groups of women who travel to other countries, such as Togo or the metropolis of Lagos in Nigeria, to find work in hairdressing or traditional medicine and remain away from their families for lengthy periods of time. In an interview with Olivier Barlet, Aïssa Maïga, the Malian-Senegalese director, notes that the Fulani Wodaabi people stay true to their character of somewhat liberated traditions when it comes to women. For example, it would not be customary to allow groups of Tuareg women to leave the family to seek work and then return.[1]

The film's narrative centres around the life of 14-year-old Houlaye Yidimama, whose mother Jowol, her activist Aunt Souri, and another female relative are shown walking away from Tatiste in order to find work; Houlaye's father must also undertake long journeys away from the family to find pastures for his herd.

Like many other girls of her age, Houlaye must take on the responsibility of caring for her siblings while her parents are away, but she too has to leave the younger children on their own when she and other girls her age make lengthy treks with donkeys to fetch water. As a result, teenage girls are missing out on education. When her aunt Souri returns to the village, she campaigns to have a deep well drilled and asks the schoolteacher to write a petition letter.

The borehole in Tatiste would be drilled 125 metres down into the Iullemeden Aquifer, a subterranean geological formation of water in porous rock that can be as deep as 600 metres. It extends horizontally far below ground across several countries, including Niger, Mali and Nigeria, and, to a lesser extent, in Algeria and Benin, which have unconnected Paleozoic aquifers.

The Amman Imman, Water is Life, NGO financed the deep drilling and is committed over the long term to the ecological restoration of marshlands and grasslands in the Azawagh region. The film's script was co-written by the director with the humanitarian ethnographer Ariane Kirtley, who founded the Amman Imman: Water is Life NGO in 2006. Connecticut-based Kirtley described the larger scale of the drilling project, intended to serve the region:

> Our hydraulic projects will help re-establish seventy percent of the marshy forest, as well as the fauna and flora, and also at least fifty percent of the pasture area. They are going to allow the reforestation of indigenous trees through agroforestry.[2]

The last scenes of the film show the completed deep drilling project and the formerly nomadic children, who had to forgo bathing during the drought, revelling in the spurting water.

The Fulani Wodaabe people are known for their festival, Guérewole, held after the rainy season, when young men finely dress and ornament themselves, engage in ecstatic dancing and stand in line to allow the young women to select from among them.

Les films du losange production company provides a detailed pedagogical dossier (in French) that includes geographical and climate change data.[3]

Simon Coulibaly Gillard, *Aya*, France/Belgium, 2021, 91 Minutes

There are some 1,500 inhabitants on Grand Lahou, a sandy spit that is part of the sand barrier in the Ivory Coast's coastal lagoon system. It lies about 150 kilometres west of Abidjan, near the delta mouth of the Bandama River, which debouches into the Gulf of Guinea. The Lahou village is all but washed away due to perpetual erosion by the sea, the deleterious effects of an upriver hydroelectric dam, as well as by climate change that has caused sea levels to rise and the river mouth to migrate. The villagers are constantly obliged to deconstruct their thatch and bamboo homes and move them further inland. Even the cemetery must be relocated, grave by grave. In the film, an elder points out the acceleration in erosion and recalls how, in his lifetime, the cemetery was once a lengthy walk away, but it is now at the beach. (See Figure 6.1.)

Aya is a docufiction feature film and is also the name of the protagonist, (Marie-Josée Degny Kokora), an Avikam girl in her early teens who lives with her recently widowed mother (Patricia Egnabayou) and baby brother (Eli Kokora) in Lahou-Kpanda village. She and her mother sell dried fish at the market, and Aya helps care for her brother. Aya's fervent wish is to continue living as her mother has on their ever-diminishing island, which was at one time a peninsula, a locale with no electricity, roads and few prospects.

As much as the film's theme is a reversal of youth wishing to move to a metropolis, it evokes the ravages of climate change and coastal erosion. The camera follows Aya's insouciant daily life in a coastal fishing village and captures vivid scenes of idyllic coastal landscapes: endless beaches and mangrove lagoons, in sunny and sometimes stormy, tumultuous weather. It contrasts to the relentless coastal erosion that has forced the villagers to make difficult decisions about their future away from Lahou-Kpanda. Aya slowly comes to realize that departure is inevitable. The family has to face relocating the remains of the family's father and husband, a fisherman lost at sea, from the cemetery, that will soon disappear. In a solemn scene, Aya is filmed placing a miniature fishing craft on his sandy grave.

Seemingly untroubled, Aya watches neighbouring villagers deconstruct their homes, first removing their roofs, then each wall, then the light wood frames, which they load onto barges that float them to new sites. She observes the families' carefree teamwork as they move their homes, and when she sees her childhood friend and almost-boyfriend Junior (Junior Asse) and his family pack their home onto barges and leave, she realizes that departure looms.

Nearly all of the inhabitants of Vieux Lahou have relocated to the new village, Grand Lahore, founded in 1973 and located to the north across the Tagba Lagoon. The site of the old village continues to be washed away. Aya's

Figure 6.1 Ivory Coast, Lahou-Kpanda, courtesy Open Street Map. (Film referenced: *Aya*.)

mother, mildly exasperated with her daughter, decides to send her to stay with an aunt in Abidjan in the hope that she'll take advantage of educational opportunities, and lectures her on the importance of staying on the right road and keeping her self-respect.

The film's epilogue shows Aya in Abidjan exploring urban teenage night-life, dancing and partying. And there is a slight nod to the recently re-released Jean Rouch short film, *La Goumbé des Noceurs* (The Goumbé of the Young Revellers, 1965), which features a community support association for primarily male rural migrants working in Abidjan, who gave open-air, traditional goumbé dance and drumming performances.[4] However, Aya has no corresponding Lahou peer support group. Late one night, disenchanted with the jostling on the dance floor, she leaves a noisy party, and slightly disoriented, she wanders off into the night through Abidjan's roaring traffic to find a view of the seashore, alone but accompanied nonetheless, *quand même*, by her small documentary crew.

The director's docufiction approach was to shoot the film in the location of the eroding village of Lahou itself. In various interviews, he has said that it was a persuasive setting in which to present 14-year-old Aya, the main character, and 'a spokesperson for the Avikam community'. He notes that it may well be the only film representing this small ethnic group of some 10,000 people (approximately 30,000 still speak Avikam) struggling with the loss of their territory, identity and language. He mentions that her casting came about when, holding her baby brother in her arms, she stepped into a panoramic frame while they were shooting a landscape scene. Similarly, Aya's mother plays her own role, and lengthy shots are located in their own family dwelling as they converse on floor mats. This empathetic approach would lengthen filming time to about six months, which also gave the director the opportunity to explore a location that would disappear. Simon Coulibaly Gillard has worked in close collaboration in all his films with his assistant Lassina Coulibaly.

In a further show of solidarity, the director organized for a generator to be set up locally to screen the film for the remaining 500 residents, who were delighted to hear their language emanating from the speakers and screen. By this time, the migrating mouth of the Bandama River was washing away the eastern flank of Vieux Lahou village. It has been reported since then that the village has been completely eroded away.[5]

Luc Marescot, *Poumon Vert et Tapis Rouge (Green Forests and the Red Carpet)*, France, 2021, 95 Minutes

Green Forests and the Red Carpet tells the story of Luc Marescot's quest to make a fictional feature film addressing reforestation at a global scale, inspired by the tropical forest research of the renowned botanist Francis Hallé. (See Figure 6.2.)

A number of films have featured Francis Hallé's phenomenal work over his long, prestigious career, including notably *Il Était Une Forêt* (2013), by director Luc Jaquet, which portrays a tropical forest with stunning landscape photography and adds animated overlay drawings in Hallé's scientific line-drawing style.

Le Radeau des Cimes (The Treetop Raft, or Canopy Raft) is a short documentary in 16 mm film (accessible at the Centre National de Recherche Scientifique (CNRS) website in a digital version of the original documentary) on a 1987 research project in Guyana, for which Francis Hallé organized a specially constructed platform to be carried by hot-air balloon and placed in the uppermost reaches of the forest branches. The dirigible poses the raft to allow researchers, harnessed for safety, to undertake scientific observation, take samples and document the tallest tropical trees.[6]

Hallé has spoken often about 'Sleeping in the Canopy', and discovering the marvellous, abundant and nocturnally luminous insect life, and how most of the species he observed have been newly documented by him.[7]

Hallé's main interest is the study of the old growth or, as he terms it, *la forêt primaire* (primary forest), and he considers what most people would call a forest to be mere plantations. He deplores the fact that almost all primary forests have disappeared, lamenting, 'It upsets me to think that in my lifetime I have seen the disappearance of the great forests of the planet'.(author's translation)[8] And in his forest talks on the Association Francis Hallé website, he says, 'When I was a young researcher in the Ivory Coast, we found very beautiful forests in the suburbs of Abidjan, now there is nothing left, just

Figure 6.2 Francis Hallé and Luc Marescot, in an Anzem tree crown in a forest in Gabon, during the filming of *Poumon vert et tapis rouge* (*Green Forest and Red Carpet*), drone photograph by Damien Chatard. Courtesy of Damien Chatard. (Film referenced: *Poumon vert et Tapis rouge – Green Forests and the Red Carpet*.)

concrete'. (author's translation).[9] Hallé estimates that for a primary forest to reach maximum biodiversity, it would take up to 700 to 1,000 years (author's translation).[10]

The director Luc Marescot first met Francis Hallé when the botanist was researching the giant trees of Madagascar

Twenty years ago I had a strange encounter with a famous botanist up in the tall trees of a tropical forest in Africa. That Botanist, Francis Hallé, was full of anger, seeing that wonderful ecosystem being cut down or burned. He was trying to fight against the logging companies. [...] He then took me on an expedition to the top of the giant trees in Madagascar; we slept there a few days, at 45 metres above ground, and it was magic, full of light, birdsong, colourful flowers, fruits and different species of animals, insects [...] I had to share the story. To help Francis in his fight to save the tropical forests I decided to do my part and write a feature film [...] to bring a message to a larger public than the one of the documentaries. One does not convince with arguments; one convinces with emotion. [...] The idea of the story is to film at least three-quarters of the movie up in the trees, at forty-five metres above ground, so that the public can discover a part of the forest it never has the opportunity to visit.[11]

The success of commercial, ecology-themed films inspired Marescot's new approach. Films such as *Avatar*, and in particular the 2006 thriller *Blood Diamond* starring Leonardo DiCaprio, a film that, despite mixed reviews, became known as an eco-thriller and succeeded in raising widespread awareness of the extent of corruption and lawlessness connected to the diamond-extraction industry, particularly as related to child soldiers. Marescot said that the film had an impressive impact on the market, and caused diamond sales to drop 15 per cent, despite the value of diamonds being artificially inflated by various marketing strategies and restricting supply.

Green Forests and the Red Carpet tracks Marescot's multi-pronged strategy to support Francis Hallé's endeavours to save the world's forests. Co-written with the wildlife film director Guillaume Maidatchevsky, Marescot pitches the script as an eco-thriller to well-known producers and A-list actors such as DiCaprio and Juliette Binoche. The most ingenious aspect of his film is the do-it-yourself approach. At each stage of the film, he looks for advice on how to take the next step forward and follows through.

It is a well-paced documentary that shows the director systematically researching and contacting influential individuals in the industry and following their suggestions step-by-step, covering a great variety of related sectors, sub-industries and artisanal professions. He explores a non-digital special effects studio where simulated cloud pattern effects are created using large transparent glass water tanks and ink drops. He takes an acting class, visits a distributor, flies to Hollywood to deposit his script at the Writers' Guild in Los Angeles, and attends the Berlin and Cannes Film Festivals. The script has yet to be filmed but was novelized as *Le Botaniste* (2022) by Jean-Luc Bizien in the eco-thriller genre.[12]

Malam Saguirou, *Solaire Made in Africa,* Niger, 2017, 67 Minutes

The documentary film *Solaire Made in Africa* demonstrates the continuing relevance of direct solar technologies that were first put into practice by the physicist professor Abdou Moumouni Dioffo in Niger in the 1960s. (See Figure 6.3.)

In the opening scene, a group of ten women are gathered at a well. An older woman reminisces about advanced technologies of an earlier era: a solar-panel-powered motor, which at one time had drawn water up and distributed it through six spigots with taps that provided drinking water. There were also additional faucets and basins supplying water for animals to drink, as well as a solar-powered mill for grinding millet.

In succeeding scenes, the solar energy specialist Professor Albert Wright, Dioffo's former pupil and then collaborator, lectures at the Centre National de l'energie solaire (CNES, formerly the Office nigérienne de l'energie solaire, ONERSOL), on direct solar energy and explains the simplicity of the technology's principles, which lend themselves perfectly to Niger's climatic conditions of heat and direct sunlight. He guides the camera through the interior and exterior of the ONERSOL building, which was designed by Professor Dioffo in collaboration with the Hungarian-born, France-based architect László Mester de Parajd.[13]

The ONERSOL research centre still operates, although its funding was cut about a decade after it was built in 1979. The wall structure is composed of thick canted double walls, with vertical ventilation shafts that circulate and exhaust heated air upwards through the roof, to provide a natural cooling system appropriate for the Niamey climate. It was intended as a prototype for public buildings and although unusually well adapted to the climate, the design was not adopted for other buildings at the time. As participants in the documentary asserted, it was in part because these sustainable innovations in solar energy and architecture were ahead of their time, as were many innovative sustainable innovations of the era. There were also capitalization issues, but the innovations will never be obsolete. If sustainable building techniques, based on and informed by Niger's vernacular architecture and solar research in the 1970s, were to be incorporated into urban buildings to be constructed

Figure 6.3 Niger, Niamey, former site of Maison Tropicale, and site of the ONERSOL building, courtesy Open Street Map. (Film referenced: *Solaire Made in Africa.*)

today, they would significantly reduce their energy consumption, as they would have when they were developed, it is a matter of finding the political will to promote energy efficiency.

Towards the end of the film, Professor Albert Wright holds an animated discussion with distinguished guests at an official dinner, during which he gives a demonstration of the use of direct heat to cook a meal. Professor Wright energetically argues, from a scientific perspective, against investing in nuclear power and advocates direct solar energy systems as the most cost-effective and sustainable option.

Short Ecological Documentaries

Anjali Nayar, *Oil and Water*, Kenya/Canada, 2018, 13 minutes

Oil and Water is a short documentary film summarizing the complex and conflicting interests in the Turkana region of northern Kenya that have arisen since the discovery of oil in the region and the arrival of a British oil company, Tullow, to exploit it. It has also had severe repercussions on the role local women play in the community due to the oil company's monopolization of the area's resources and limiting their access to a scarce water supply.

The film documents a village in crisis. The oil company had negotiated with the government and the men of the village and made decisions in which the women had no say and were not even aware of until they discovered that their traditional responsibility for bringing water to the village for human and livestock consumption had been affected and were no longer able access water at all. As a result, the women began to organize in order to have some say in the water supply.

Shortly after the discovery of oil and the start of its operations, Tullow Oil, based in Lokichar, Kenya, experienced financial difficulties and was unable to meet its commitments, it reneged on its promise to supply water to the village. The area is drought-prone and had been devastated by prolonged drought when four consecutive rainy seasons failed: the rainy season, known as the long rains or *masika,* should occur from mid-March to May, and the *vuli,* a shorter rainy season, from November to December.

As the rainy seasons had failed again in northern Kenya, the film documents Turkana women: tall, striking figures usually wearing their traditional stacked beaded necklaces, rallying to discuss and organize themselves to take action.[14] All the while, Tullow's corporate website has kept up an optimistic outlook, which is belied by continued financial ups and downs as well as being sued by a group of Kenyans for environmental damage.

Marlyse Awa Yotomane, *Lucie,* Central African Republic, 2019, 25 Minutes

This short documentary follows the endless, strenuous work in the daily life of a 38-year-old rural woman, Lucie Patricia Yagandia, work that is typically undertaken by women in rural Central African Republic. Lucie lives with her husband, Edgar Kongbo and their children in the village of Socada, near Sibut, the capital of the Kémo prefecture, which is 185 km north of Bangui, the country's capital city.

Lucie is first seen bantering with her husband, Edgar, as they both set off for the day. She walks some distance to a farmer's field to bargain with the farmer for tomatoes. She wins the deal and buys a mass of tomatoes that she carries home in a large bowl on her head. When she has sorted them, she sets out again to dig for cassava roots and carries an even heavier load in a wide bowl, including the machete, on her head, taking the load to a stream to wash; she then peels, chops and spreads the roots out to dry. Lucie gathers, sweeps and cleans, as well as helps to build. In the bush, she gathers thatching straw into a bundle larger than her body size and, then, balancing it on her head, traverses a tree trunk as she fords a stream.

In lighter moments, she prepares an alcoholic beverage with two female friends and serves the brew to a group of men while Bangana-Ngouli, a musician, plays a stringed instrument and, accompanied by a drummer, sings a long, improvised and fragmented lyric that makes scattered references to regional conflicts. There is only ambient sound on the soundtrack. Despite the dark lyrics, Lucie dances along to the music as she serves the men.

In a long sequence, Lucie sits under a tree with her husband and asks him playfully if he has bought her presents, but he smiles and dodges the question. She smiles too as she sings teasingly, ad-libbing the lyrics, 'When I was single, life was beautiful. What drove me to marry you?' Gesturing, she continues, 'Don't break my heart with your bad behaviour'.

As she sings, she is still smiling.

Shortly before the end of the film (at 20 minutes), a hand-pushed cart delivers earthen bricks to form the walls of the house on a site in Tokowel. Edgar is filmed making a mortar of earth and water and suggests she could help him mix it. Lucie replies, 'Where am I going to find a shovel? I'm too tired'.

When he shoots back, 'You're not just here to talk'. Lucie repeats, 'I'm tired from working so hard'.

The roof structure is in place, and next the straw thatch is attached.

At the end of the film, Lucie is seen digging and shovelling earth into a metal container, and she returns to her song, a cappella, 'What drove me to marry you?' And as she shovels, she sings, 'Women dig the ground just like men'.[15]

Soussaba Cissé, *Bogo Ja, (L'âme de la terre, The Soul of the earth)*, Mali, 2020, 52 Minutes

The director, Soussaba Cissé, has been involved in the making of several short films that often address controversial social issues such as excision, migration and war. She is the daughter of director Souleymane Cissé, and has worked as a crew member on some of his films, such as the docufiction *O Ka* (*Notre Maison*, 2016).[16] (See Figure 6.4.)

Set in the village of Siby, some 50 kilometres from Bamako, *Bogo Ja* is about the ancestral culture and tradition of Malian rural women and their responsibilities in maintaining earthen homes in Mali. The film addresses women's roles in the upkeep, decoration and seasonal maintenance of traditional housing and who engage collectively as mural artists working with the exterior wall of each house so that the common space at the scale of the village becomes an integrated array of pigmented and patterned large-scale abstract murals.

This short documentary film follows an annual five-day event held every April in Siby and documents the work of five women in the village, who are among some four hundred contestants engaging in the collective mural practice, each competing to maintain the exterior walls of her dwelling using ancient techniques that involve hand-rubbed earthen parging. Women often travel long distances to source and collect unusual earth pigments, gathering samples for the purpose of creating individual designs, inventive motifs and organic curvilinear and geometric patterns in a range of colours. The painted surfaces include the enclosures and granaries as well as the walls of traditional dwellings.[17]

Seidou Samba Touré, *Massiiba (le mal d'un people)*, Burkina Faso, 2021, 62 Minutes

Filmed in Gorom-Gorom, in the north of Burkina Faso, the documentary *Massïiba (le mal d'un people)* by the filmmaker Seidou Samba Touré chronicles the effects of unrest, violence and political instability in Burkina Faso's northern provinces, that have come to be called the Red Zone. (See Figure 6.5.)

Seidou Samba Touré was born in Gorom-Gorom, and initially the film was to feature his childhood friend Boukari, a truck driver. But in 2018, Boukari was ambushed and has not been seen since. His disappearance was linked to the unrest in the region that has been called an invisible war in a news blackhole. After attending a workshop in 2015 on countering violent extremism, run by the American embassy in Ougagadougou, Touré began shooting many hours of footage, and between 2016 and 2020, he filmed in

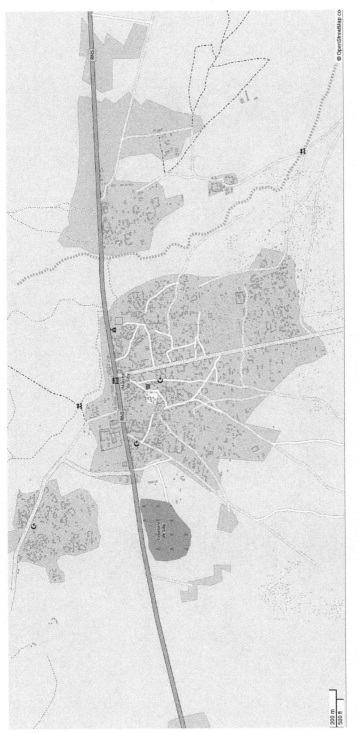

Figure 6.4 Mali, Siby, courtesy Open Street Map. (Film referenced: *Bɔgɔ Ja.*)

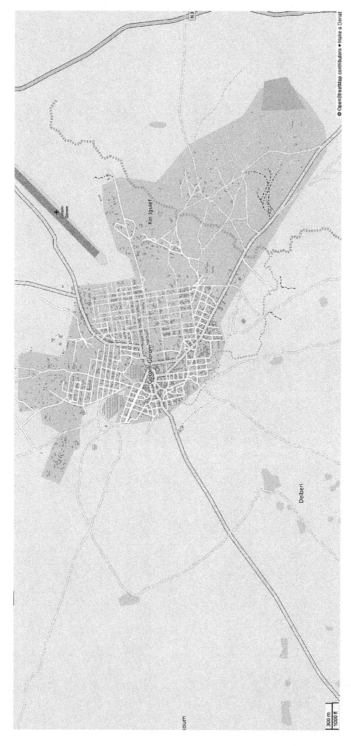

Figure 6.5 Burkina Faso, Gorom-Gorom, courtesy Open Street Map. (Film referenced: *Massiiba [le mal d'un people].*)

the once peaceful towns of Fada N'Gourma, Gorom-Gorom, Nongana in the savannah and the desert city of Oursi, in the north of Burkina Faso. Favouring first-hand accounts, he compiled numerous interviews and conversations with educators, a guide from the Oursi museum, an elderly woman and many others, and the film demonstrates his empathetic commitment to listening to detail. The narrative takes the form of a letter to his missing friend.[18]

The documentary is on-the-ground investigative journalism that probes the rarely filmed effects of political instability on the daily lives of inhabitants of a politically and climatically challenged region, who live in daily fear and are powerless in the face of the frightening realities of insecurity, including random armed kidnapping, hence the title *Massiiba*, an Arabic word for le mal in French or misfortune.[19]

Notes

1 Aïssa Maïga, 'Aïssa Maïga, Le Grand entretien avec Aïssa Maïga', interview by Olivier Barlet, *Africultures*, 21 April 2022 (accessed 12 December 2023) https://africultures.com/le-grand-entretien-avec-aissa-maiga-15351/. Comments from the interview with Aïssa Maïga: 'J'ai choisi le Niger car je voulais le contact d'une communauté peuhl et que j'avais appris que les femmes wodaabé étaient amenées à faire des exodes assez réguliers en direction des pays riches de la sous-région, devenant ainsi des piliers économiques dans leur communauté. Sur place, j'ai découvert de fortes personnalités. Les femmes wodaabé partent seules entre femmes, ce qui serait inenvisageable chez les Touaregs proches, qui n'envisagent pas de faire travailler leurs femmes.' (I chose Niger because I wanted contact with a Fulani community and I had learnt that Wodaabe women made regular journeys to wealthier countries of the sub-region, and becoming economic forces in their community. While there I discovered strong personalities. Wodaabe women leaving with other women: that would be unimaginable with the Touregs, who wouldn't think of allowing their women to work in this way.) (author's translation).
2 Ariane Kirtley, 'Portrait of Initiator of *Marcher sur l'eau*, and "PRECIOUS WATER!" challengelaureate', interviewed by FAMAE, *Medium*, 9 July 2019 (accessed 10 December 2023) https://famae.medium.com/portrait-of-ariane-kirtley-initiator-of-marcher-sur-leau-and-precious-water-9a3bc612f14b. See also https://arianekirtley.com/
3 Aïssa Maïga, *Marcher sur l'eau*, Dossier pédagogique (accessed 12 December 2023) https://filmsdulosange.com/film/marcher-sur-leau/.
4 Jean Rouch, director, *La Goumbé des jeunes noceurs* (*The Goumbé of the Young Revelers*) (Ivory Coast, Les Films des Pléiades, 1965, 27 min.) https://icarusfilms.com/if-goumbe, Ivory Coast associations for young people's club meetings in Abidjan.
5 François Hume-Ferkatadji, special correspondent, à Lahou-Kpanda, 'Côte d'Ivoire: les habitants de Lahou-Kpanda découvrent *Aya*, film sur leur village et leur culture', *RFI (Radio France Internationale)*, 6 March 2023 (accessed 10 August 2023) https://www.rfi.fr/fr/afrique/20230306-c%C3%B4te-d-ivoire-les-habitants-de-lahou-kpanda-d%C3%A9couvrent-aya-film-sur-leur-village-et-leur-culture.

6 Francis Hallé and Alain Robert Devez, *Le Radeau des cimes.* France/French Guyane, 1987, 16 mm. film, 26 min. CNRS Images (*Centre National de Recherche Scientifique*) (accessed 8 August 2023) https://images.cnrs.fr/video/141.

7 Francis Hallé, *Le radeaux des cimes… dormir sur la canopée.* Ushuaïa TV, 2022 (accessed 9 September 2023) https://www.youtube.com/watch?v=PRipmR0uC_Y. See also: Francis Hallé, Quatorze épisodes sur la forêt par Francis Hallé, Association Francis Hallé, 2020, ép.01, Présentation de Francis Hallé, 4.03 min (accessed 9 October 2023) https://www.youtube.com/playlist?list=PLz9jLq2Rm3h3eGrJZJqR0rjdXS 6tJf4ja. Francis Hallé, '…ça m'émeut beaucoup de penser que dans la durée de ma vie j'ai vu disparaître toutes les grandes forêts primaires de la terre.' (author's translation).

8 Francis Hallé, 'Aux arbres citoyens!', *Radio-France* 8 November 2022, 54 min (accessed 9 October 2023) https://www.radiofrance.fr/franceinter/podcasts/la-terre-au-carre /la-terre-au-carre-du-mardi-08-novembre-2022-6632297.

9 Francis Hallé, 'Se libérer du règne de la mesure et renouer avec la sensibilité', *Reporterre*, 24 May 2021 (accessed 9 October 2023) https://reporterre.net/Francis -Halle-Se-liberer-du-regne-de-la-mesure-et-renouer-avec-la-sensibilite. Quand j'étais jeune chercheur en Côte d'Ivoire, on trouvait encore de très belles forêts dans la ban-lieue d'Abidjan, maintenant il n'y a plus rien, juste du béton. (author's translation).

10 Ibid.

11 Luc Marescot, *The Botanist, an Ecological Thriller; a Story with Deep Roots* (accessed 10 September 2023) https://luc-marescot.com/films/the-botanist/.

12 Jean-Luc Bizien, *Le Botanist* (Paris: Fayard, 2022), adapted from the screenplay by Luc Marescot and Guillaume Maidatchevsky.

13 László Mester de Parajd, Alsatian architect, Solar Energy Research Centre, ONERSOL Office Nigérien de l'énergie solaire, Niger Niamey, 'Aga Khan Award Shortlisted project', ARCHNET, 1981 (accessed 21 June 2021) https://www.archnet .org/sites/332.

14 Anjali Nayar, *Oil and Water* (accessed 21 June 2023) https://www.cineground.com/ credit-oil-in-water.

15 Marlyse Awa Yotomane *Lucie* (accessed 10 October 2023) The film can be viewed on https://vimeo.com/443299516. See also: Marlyse Awa Yotomane, *Lucie*, The entire film is posted (accessed 10 October 2023) https://www.ateliersvaran.com/fr/cinema-theque/lucie-yotomane_1883.

16 Souleymane Cissé, *O Ka* (*Notre Maison*), Mali, 2015, 110 min. https://www.film-doc-umentaire.fr/4DACTION/w_fiche_film/45763_0, Soussaba Cissé. https://www .legroupeouest.com/les-auteures/soussaba-cisse/.

17 Soussaba Cissé, *Bogo Ja, l'Âme de la terre (Mali, BankO Productions, 2020).* http://www .lussasdoc.org/film-bogo_ja-1,53926.html?locale=en_US, Extracts Soussaba Cissé, *Bogo Ja.* https://vimeo.com/486435287. Soussaba Cissé, https://www.legroupeouest .com/les-auteures/soussaba-cisse/.

18 Sophie Douce, 'Au Burkina Faso, l'ode à la résilience du cinéaste Seidou Samba Touré', *Le Monde*, 23 October 2021 (accessed 8 June 2023) https://www.lemonde.fr/ afrique/article/2021/10/23/au-burkina-faso-l-ode-a-la-resilience-du-cineaste-seidou -samba-toure_6099630_3212.html. See also: Seidou Samba Touré, *Massiiba, le mal d'un people,* teaser, https://vimeo.com/536897550. Seidou Samba Touré, *Massiiba, le mal d'un people* https://vimeo.com/532453284. A message from Seidou Samba Touré, *Massiiba, le mal d'un* people (accessed 30 June 2024) https://vimeo.com/532453284.

19 Ibid.

CONCLUSION FOR UPCOMING GENERATIONS

Here, it has less to do with thinking of the city as a superstructure (which it certainly is) than as a production of meaning or direction [sens] whose significations inform our social and political reality, but, above all, our imaginaries and our projections.

Felwine Sarr[1]

Most architects, urbanists, landscape architects and designers broadcast and disseminate their work by means of public speaking tours. In recent years, this practice has been augmented by recorded versions that can be streamed anytime and often are embedded into their company websites. Rwandan architect Christian Benimana, who leads the Africa Studio in the Boston-based architectural practice Mass Design, gave a talk to a large audience in Arusha, Tanzania, on August 2017, as part of the popular Ted Talk series.

In his talk, entitled 'The Next Generation of Architects and Designers', Benimana speaks of the African continent's urgent near-future needs to match the population growth, which he estimated would require 700,000,000 sustainable housing units, more than 300,000 schools and 85,000 medical clinics to be built by 2050. He translated those numbers into seven medical clinics, 25 schools and about 60,000 housing units per day. Benimana is optimistic that this massive task can be achieved sustainably by African architects who understand the landscape and the population's needs. He illustrates his talk with examples of his own work, such as a new prototype project, the Kasungu Maternity Village, attached to the Kasungu District Hospital in Malawi. Completed in 2015, it provides shelter and antenatal care for expectant mothers from their thirty-sixth week, which helps reduce maternity casualties.[2]

He also presented the work of other architects in the Ted Talk, which includes a prototype project by the Nigerian architect Kunlé Adeyemi, whose Amsterdam- and Lagos-based design and development practice NLÉ proposed the Makoko Floating School project of A-frame triangular structures on barges to serve as schools and community centres for Makoko's floating informal settlement in Lagos,[3] and Diébédo Francis Kéré in Burkina Faso, who designed the Lycée Schorge secondary school (completed 2018) in Kougoudou, a region with a population of about 200,000. The school was built from locally sourced materials using local construction processes and involves and serves the local community.[4]

In addition to Benimana's concise list of innovative prototypes for architecture in Africa, there are a number of contemporary architects and designers across the world who are involved in creating inventive, sustainable buildings and environments, such as the architect Manual Herz, who designed the Tambacoumba Paediatric and Maternity Hospital in eastern Senegal. Notable for its use of curvilinear forms constructed in clay brick, it was completed in 2021. The project was commissioned and funded by the Connecticut-based Josef and Annie Albers Foundation with the Le Korsa NGO.[5]

Could these innovative building prototypes and showcase projects that are often sited in rural, open natural landscapes expand and integrate into contemporary cities? And what kinds of public spaces and infrastructural systems can bring these new built forms together into new cities?

One approach to answering such questions is to look at proposals by emerging architects and designers as a conclusion in a more speculative form.

Speculative Urbanism: Recent Design Research Proposals Sited in African Cities

During certain visits to various African cities and observing their appearance and rhythms, tendencies of urbanization, and their atmosphere, the same feeling constantly rose up from within me that they were all searching for a face, that they hadn't yet exactly found their own true identity, that they were being tossed about by the winds, subjected to the dynamism of a certain form or a certain desire of modernity, caught between a bygone past and future whose enigmas were yet to be deciphered (Felwine Sarr).[6]

In the early part of the century, architectural education continued to evolve away from Eurocentric canons, while a sequence of events, including the pandemic and geopolitical upheavals have intensified the call for forward-facing action on diversifying contemporary design and urban research and are propelling a shift away from narrower architectural and urban design traditions towards an informed perspective that recognizes the imperative of responding to climate change, and is guided by local knowledge and current research.

The eminent urbanist and engineer Daniel Biau, with decades of extensive African experience, enumerates a series of ten points that he considers
high-priority agenda items in urbanism that apply to the African continent,
beginning with the transformation of digital work, or telework, and the inten-
sification of remote work since the pandemic. Nairobi-based Biau considers
one potential effect to be the decline of the traditional central business centre,
as white-collar workers no longer need to commute to a downtown office for a
five-day work week, a trend that may lead to obsolete high-rise, often glass-clad
office towers. The twenty-first-century city may reflect changing work and
commuting patterns, with more integrated, mixed neighbourhoods. Transit
(in the African context, often a mini-bus network) would reflect this change.
Biau's list calls for more localized supply chains, and more state involvement
in urban planning. Another plank in his platform calls for a balanced city
network in the region, which he sums up with the slogan, 'medium-size cities versus megacities'. Many of the world's largest cities are dysfunctional in
terms of housing costs, transit, sustainability and overall affordability, and
lower-income citizens seek alternatives to the labour market in very large,
dense cities.[7]

In the context of climate crises, a key example among the many ideas
for sustainable and green cities, recycled or upcycled cities, or pedestrian-
oriented bicycle and car-free cities is the sponge city concept, an idea developed and put into practice by the Chinese urbanist and landscape architect
Kongjian Yu and his company Turenscape to improve river and wetland systems to mitigate flooding and excessive storm water runoff. Other areas of
transformation would involve new ideas to reinforce landscape infrastructure
to prevent flooding and mitigate drought. The multidisciplinary design approach of Kongjian Yu advocates for the creation of what he calls sponge
cities, ecosystem infrastructure that can absorb flash downpours. He has
recently called for a Sponge planet, to ward off large-scale climate change
effects, not only to prevent flooding but also to replenish aquifers whose
depletion has caused damaging subsidence. Another area of his interest is in
zones where salt and freshwater meet, and he has made a case for sponge city
solutions for brackish water.[8]

Examining the research undertaken and the theses written by recent gradu-
ates, who are mostly either native to Africa or have lived there, helps to gauge
how innovative architectural and urban practices might be applied in several
African countries. The following paragraphs look at recent research and graduate projects that demonstrate a fresh engagement with architecture, urban
design and the environment in relation to some of the cities and settlements
from north to south on the continent and include a variety of thesis proposals
and discussions by Laila Hossam Abdallah, Cairo, Egypt; Ogbe David Ogbe,

Lagos; Folusho Ashish Afun-Ogidan, Makoko floating settlement in Lagos, Nigeria; Chinenye Ogbu, the Igboland region of Nigeria; Deepakshi Mittal, Kibera, Nairobi, Kenya; Amal Dirie, Somaliland; Meryem Chahboum, Rabat, Morocco; Victor Zagabe, Democratic Republic of Congo; and Anna Longrigg, Capetown, South Africa. Undergraduate projects include Zoya Khan, Nairobi, Kenya and Nothando Bhila, Harare, Zimbabwe. Each project highlights some of the challenges undertaken by architectural practices today. (See Figure C.1)

These research and design projects demonstrate the contemporary socio-cultural and socio-political interests that typically incorporate a post-colonial critique. One of the most far-reaching of these projects, 'Nomadic Passage: Water Conservation and Land Preservation', (2020), by Amal Dirie, addresses issues on territory, settlement, traditional cultures and property.[9] Her minutely detailed research documents nomadic Somali housing traditionally built by women and how they serve as temporary domestic environments. Her refined drawing and photography illustrate the key elements of the process of hut construction and dismantlement. Dirie raises many questions about cities and sustainability in Somaliland, where about half of the population follows a nomadic way of life, and where scarcity of resources, food insecurity and land stewardship capacity resulting from drought have dangerously impacted a semi-nomadic population. Her design proposal,

Figure C.1 Amal Dirie, 'Nomadic Passage: Water Conservation and Land Preservation', 2020, Nomadic Huts, Rural Outskirts of Hargeisa, Somaliland, photograph by Amal Dirie. Fig 2.19 p. 88. (Work referenced: Amal Dirie.)

oriented towards the collective space of a well, also incorporates the cultural practice of storytelling in a built form that integrates with the landscape.

The impact of modern architecture and urbanism in the colonial context is a critical theme in Meryem Chahboun's thesis, 'Echoes of Decolonization, From North Africa to Europe: Questioning the Trip Back Home', which focusses on the years between 1912 and 1970. Her work discusses the colonial-built city centre of Rabat, Morocco, and how the impact of French colonial urbanism prepared the ground for transnational modernist projects and discourse. She sees in it exchanges of ideas that are not sufficiently recognized and advocates further interrogation of colonial urbanism, noting examples such as the work of Candilis Woods Architects, whose experiments in 'practice ideas developed in North Africa', were themes framed as the 'restructuring of everyday life around postwar Fordist capitalist trends', such as the 'control of domesticity, politicization of space, and designing for the masses'.[10]

The acute urban consequences of building the new administrative city outside Cairo is the subject of the thesis by Laila Hossam Abdalla, entitled 'A Tale of Two Cities: Re-Imagining Tahrir Square's Muggamaa Complex(e)', (2020). Her project obliquely criticizes the new ex-urban American- and Chinese-designed and constructed New Administrative Capital before turning her attention to focus on, and to value the immense Muggamaa building on Tahrir Square, slated to be emptied once the new capital is completed, along with some 76 buildings in the once lively urban context.[11]

Ogbe David Ogbe's thesis, 'Temple Of Afrobeat(s): Re-Imagination of The New Afrika Shrine', (2020), examines the legacies of the exceptional musician and performer Fela Kuti, who, along with drummer and composer Tony Allen, was the originator of Afrobeat which evolved into Afrobeats. The introduction to Ogbe's research project is devoted to an overview of Nigerian music and to the life of Fela Kuti, one of Nigeria's most influential musicians and political activists of the twentieth century. The research begins with Fela Kuti's family origins, in the town of Abeo-kuta, in Ogun state of Nigeria, and in particular the influence of Kuti's activist mother, Funmilayo Kuti. He positions the musical implication of the Kuti legacy within the political events in Nigeria. His activism led to imprisonment and many arrests, and his establishment of Afrika Shrine was a serious thorn in the Nigerian government's flesh and was closed down in 1977. Ogbe discusses the founding of the Afrika Shrine, which was re-established in Ikeja in Lagos, then rebuilt in 2000 by Fela Kuti's musician son, Femi Kuti. Since Fela Kuti was introduced to activism by his mother and the teachings of Kwame Nkrumah of Ghana, Ogbe's research emphasizes the 'Pan-African socialist message of entertainment to Afro-conscious political and social enlightenment'. Ogbe's fieldwork took him to visit the New Afrika Shrine in January 2020, leading him to decide to expand on the socio-political ideals of Afrobeats and enlarge his design proposal, aiming for a full, elaborate public community programme, including educating and rehabilitating youth through contemporary music, and social-political programming of the Shrine as a community centre.[12] (See Figure C.2)

Makoko is a unique district in the metropolis of Lagos and is studied in Folusho Ashish Afun-Ogidan's thesis, entitled 'Venice of Lagos – Reviving the fishing culture in Makoko through Aquaponics', (2019). The research addresses the complex socio-political status and the ecologies of Makoko's informal floating city on the Lagos lagoon, as well as its viability within the mega-city of Lagos, Nigeria. He emphasizes its connections with the fishing and lumber markets of the Ómó forest reserve. Taking inspiration from the well-known example of the floating school designed by Kunlée Adeyemi of NLÉ as a significant local precedent, Afun-Ogidan proposes a lightweight floating aquaponic farm and farmhouse, as a prototype for Makoko.[13]

The landscape of the Igboland region of Nigeria is analysed, sited and presented with detailed designs in 'Red Earth: Shaping the Igbo Family Compound' (2022), a thesis by Chinenye Ogbu on the transformation of the family compound housing typology. The research looks at traditional Igbo family buildings, large structures set in enclosed compounds in the Enugu

Figure C.2 David Ogbe, 'The Temple Of Afrobeat(s): Re-Imagination of The New Afrika Shrine', 2020. Festival Experience, digital render by David Ogbe, p. 119, Fig 4.61. (Work referenced: David Ogbe.)

landscape, and examines the effects of British colonialism and post-colonial restructuring. Her design proposal updates these forms and adapts them to the present.[14]

The recycling economy of the improvised city is the subject of Deepakshi Mittal's thesis proposal, 'Waste as Resource: Recycling housing components in the informal settlement of Kibera, Nairobi, Kenya' (2023). Taking the unbuilding, disassembling and scavenging practices as already embedded in the realities of constructing self-built housing in Kibera, and following AbdouMaliq Simone's ideas about the ecologies of human occupancy, Mittal analyses the ways in which microscale interventions could improve the viability of smaller structures and proposes a site next to a school for a reclaimed materials depot to store recycled building materials with facilities for related community services.[15]

A systematic mapping of residual apartheid characterizes the thesis research by Anna Longrigg, 'Practices of Furtive Commoning in the [Post] Apartheid, [Post]Colonial City of Cape Town, South Africa', (2020), demonstrates the persistence of racial and financial segregation that is maintained in both informal and upper-income gated communities, and assesses through mapping, how urban forms 'perpetuate colonial and apartheid era patterns of socio-spatial segregation'.[16]

In another approach, Victor Zagabe's thesis, 'Tuning Monuments', (2020), articulates further criticism of the post-colonial and post-independence eras. His work examines what he describes as the dubious 'historicity of monuments to authoritarian regimes' and criticizes 'historically inaccurate monuments that censor and sanitize reality'. He further proposes counter monuments in the context of the historic colonial relationship between the Democratic Republic of Congo and Belgium, as well as addressing the 'process of radical decolonization known as Zairianization'.[17]

Two undergraduate students have programmed and proposed exemplary design projects for performance spaces in inner-city parks. Nothando Bhila's proposed design for an Afro-jazz band shell is sited in the city centre in Harare Gardens, Harare, Zimbabwe, while Zhoya Khan's design for a studio and performance venue for a popular local group is sited in Nairobi's two-and-a-half-thousand-acre (1,000 hectares) Karura Forest, one of the largest forests within a city's limits in the world.

The fresh insights and observations in the students' research undertaken by these upcoming architects and their aspirations for their chosen sites not only show an empathetic, anticipatory perspective, but also a developed and balanced post-colonial critique. In each situation studied, their photography, drawings and diagrams, as well as their overall work shows their sensitivity to the needs and issues affecting the greater population in Africa. In the coming era, collectively imagining and creating human settlements using digital drawing and rendering, as well as the moving image and cinematic processes, may provide an accumulation of innovative ideas for urbanists to consider and lead to more qualitative, ecological and equitable levels of human inhabitation on the African continent (and elsewhere), to better serve the planet.

Notes

1 Felwine Sarr, *Afrotopia*. Trans. Drew S. Burk and Sarah Jones-Boardman. Minneapolis and London: University of Minnesota Press, 2020, p. 104. Originally published in French as *Afrotopia*. Paris: Philippe Rey, 2022. Ici, il s'agira moins de penser la ville comme une superstructure (ce qu'elle est), mais comme une production de sens dont les significations informant sur notre réalité sociale et politique, mais surtout sur nos imaginaires et nos projections.

2 Christian Benimana, 'The Next Generation of Architects and Designers', Ted Global, August 2017 (accessed 20 December 2023) https://www.ted.com/talks/ christian_benimana_the_next_generation_of_african_architects_and_designers. See also: Mass Design, Maternity Waiting Village. Kasungu, Malawi (accessed 20 December 2023) https://massdesigngroup.org/work/design/maternity-waiting-village and Stephanie Nolan, reporting from towns and villages in western Ghana. 'More Women in Africa are using Long-acting Contraception, Changing Lives', Photographs by Nataliija Gormalova, *New York Times*, 17 June 2024 (accessed 17 June 2024), Re: Post Partum family planning, https://www.nytimes.com/2024/06/17/ health/long-acting-contraception-africa.html.

3 Kunle Adeyemi, 'The Makoko Floating School, Lagos, Nigeria', *Divisare*, 25 May 2016 (accessed 20 December 2023) https://divisare.com/projects/317757-nle-kunle -adeyemi-the-makoko-floating-school.

4 Kéré Architecture, Lycée Schorge, 2014–2016 (accessed 31 December 2023) https:// www.kerearchitecture.com/work/building/lycee-schorge.

5 Manuel Herz, Tambacounda Hospital, Tambacounda, Senegal (accessed 8 December 2023) http://www.manuelherz.com/tambacounda-hospital. See also: Josef and Anni Albers Foundation (accessed 8 December 2023) https://www.albersfoundation.org/ foundation.

6 Felwine Sarr, *Afrotopia*. Trans. Drew S. Burk and Sarah Jones-Boardman. Minneapolis and London: University of Minnesota Press, 2020, pp. 104–105.

7 Daniel Biau, 'Shifting Paradigms in Urbanism, A Contribution to the Urban Economy Forum 2020', 6 October 2020 (accessed 20 April 2024) https://danielbiau .webnode.page/news/shifting-paradigms-in-urbanism/. See also https://www.citie-salliance.org/resources/publications/global-knowledge/urban-guru-website-daniel -biau.

8 Kongjian Yu, Recipient of the Oberlander Prize for Landscape Architecture 11 November 2023 (accessed 20 May 2024) https://www.turenscape.com/en/news/ detail/449.html. See also: Anna Thoms and Stephen Köster, 'Potentials for Sponge City Implementation in Sub-Saharan Africa', *Sustainability* 14, no. 18 (September 2022): 11726. https://www.researchgate.net/profile/Stephan-Koester2?_tp=eyJjb25 0ZXh0Ijp7ImZpcnN0UGFnZSI6InB1YmxpY2F0aW9uIiwicGFnZSI6InB1Ymx pY2F0aW9uIn19 The cities of Hawassa (Ethiopia), Beira (Mozambique), Kigali

(Rwanda), Ouagadougou (Burkina Faso), and Cotonou (Benin) are examined in detail.

9 Amal Dirie, 'Nomadic Passage: Water Conservation and Land Preservation', *Master of Architecture Thesis, University of Waterloo*, *UWSpace*, 2020 (accessed 9 October 2023) https://uwspace.uwaterloo.ca/handle/10012/15787.

10 Meryem Chahboun, 'Echoes of Decolonization | From North Africa to Europe: Questioning the Trip Back Home', *Master of Architecture Thesis, University of Waterloo*, *UWSpace*, 2021 (accessed 9 October 2023) https://uwspace.uwaterloo.ca/handle/10012/17675.

11 Laila Hossam Abdalla, 'A Tale of Two Cities: Re-Imagining Tahrir Square's Muggamaa Complex(e)', *Master of Architecture Thesis, University of Waterloo*, *UWSpace*, 2020 (accessed 9 October 2023) https://uwspace.uwaterloo.ca/handle/10012/15988.

12 Ogbe David Ogbe, 'The Temple of Afrobeat(s): Re-Imagination of The New Afrika Shrine', *Master of Architecture Thesis, University of Waterloo*, *UWSpace*, 2020 (accessed 9 October 2023) https://uwspace.uwaterloo.ca/handle/10012/16292.

13 Folusho Ashish Afun-Ogidan, 'Venice of Lagos - Reviving the Fishing Culture in Makoko through Aquaponics', *Master of Architecture Thesis, University of Waterloo*, *UWSpace*, 2020 (accessed 9 October 2023) https://uwspace.uwaterloo.ca/handle/10012/15124.

14 Chinenye Ogbu, 'Red Earth: Shaping the Igbo Family Compound', *Master of Architecture thesis, University of Waterloo*, *UWSpace*, 2022 (accessed 9 October 2023) https://uwspace.uwaterloo.ca/handle/10012/18786.

15 Deepakshi Mittal, 'Waste as Resource: Recycling Housing Components in the Informal Settlement of Kibera, Nairobi, Kenya', *Master of Architecture Thesis, University of Waterloo*, *UWSpace*, 2023 (accessed 9 October 2023) https://uwspace.uwaterloo.ca/handle/10012/19867.

16 Anna Longrigg, 'Practices of Furtive Commoning in the [Post]Apartheid, [Post] Colonial City of Cape Town, South Africa',*Master of Architecture Thesis, University of Waterloo*, *UWSpace*, 2022 (accessed 9 October 2023) https://uwspace.uwaterloo.ca/handle/10012/18064.

17 Victor Zagabe, 'Tuning Monuments', *Master of Architecture thesis, University of Waterloo*, *UWSpace*, 2020 (accessed 9 October 2023) https://uwspace.uwaterloo.ca/handle/10012/15915.

BIBLIOGRAPHY

Adjaye, David. *Africa Architecture: A Photographic Survey of Metropolitan Architecture.* London: Thames & Hudson, 2011.

Agha, Menna. 'The Non-Work Of The Unimportant: The Shadow Economy of Nubian Women in Displacement Villages'. *Kohl Journal for Body and Gender Research* 5, no. 2 (Summer 2019). Accessed 15 March 2024. https://kohljournal.press/non-work -unimportant.

Bâ, Amadou Hampâté. 'La tradition orale africaine'. Documentary. Directed by Ange Casta. Series: *Un Certain Regard.* ORTF (1969). Accessed 12 October 2023. https:// www.youtube.com/watch?v=tli3rweFa48.

Barlet, Olivier. *African Cinemas: Decolonizing the Gaze.* London: Zed Books, 2000.

Baumard, Maryline. 'A Paris, l'autre bataille de Stalingrad des migrants'. *Le Monde,* 19 March 2016. Accessed 1 October 2023. https://www.lemonde.fr/societe/article/2016 /03/19/a-paris-l-autre-bataille-de-stalingrad-des-migrants_4886111_3224.html.

Binet, Jacques. 'La ville à travers le cinéma d'Afrique noire'. Special issue, *le Défi de la Ville: Spiritus* 23, no. 86 (1982): 31–43. https://www.revue-spiritus.com/portfolio/86.

Binet, Jacques and Susanna Contini. 'Urbanism and Its Expression in the African City'. *Diogenes* 24, no. 93 (1976): 11–10. Accessed 10 November 2023. https://doi .org/10.1177/039219217602409305; https://journals.sagepub.com/doi/10.1177 /039219217602409305.

Boukari-Yabara, Amzat. 'Felwine Sarr. *Afrotopia*'. *Afrique contemporaine* 1, no. 257 (2016): 150–153. Translated by Claire Stout in Cairn Info International edition (website). Accessed 12 August 2023. https://doi.org/10.3917/afco.257.0150. https://www.cairn .info/revue-afrique-contemporaine-2016-1-page-150.htm.

Corlass, Alain. 'Maison Tropicale'. *Dakar Plateau Blogspot,* 23 March 2011. Accessed 10 October 2023. https://dakarplateau.blogspot.com/2011/03/maison-tropicale -manthia-diawara.html.

Cottenet-Hage, Madeleine. 'Decolonizing Images: Soleil Ô and the Cinema of Med Hondo'. In *Cinema, Colonialism, PostColonialism, Perspectives from the French and Francophone Worlds.* Edited by Dina Sherzer. Austin: University of Texas Press, 1996, 173–187.

Dovey, Lindiwe. *African Film and Literature: Adapting Violence to the Screen.* New York: Columbia University Press, 2009.

Downing, John D.H. 'Post-Tricolor African Cinema: Toward a Richer Vision'. In *Cinema, Colonialism, PostColonialism, Perspectives from the French and Francophone Worlds.* Edited by Dina Sherzer. Austin: University of Texas Press, 1996, 188–228.

Enwezor, Okwui, et al., ed. *Under Siege: Four African Cities: Freetown, Johannesburg, Kinshasa, Lagos.* Brochure, Documenta 11_4. Stuttgart: Hatje Cantz, 2002.

Gaulme, François. 'Gabon: From Timber to Petroleum'. *Review of African Political Economy* 18, no. 51 (1991): 84–87.

Herz, Manuel, ed. In collaboration with ETH Studio Basel. *From Camp to City*. Zürich, Switzerland: Lars Muller Publishers, 2013.

Iheka, Cajetan. *African Ecomedia: Network Forms, Planetary Politics*. Durham, NC: Duke University Press, 2021.

Maja-Pearce, Adewale. 'Strewn with Loot'. *London Review of Books*, 43, no. 16 (12 August 2021). Accessed 3 January 2022. https://www.lrb.co.uk/the-paper/v43/n16/adewale -maja-pearce/strewn-with-loot.

Mandefro Belaye, Hone. 'Ethiopia has one of Africa's Most Ambitious Housing Policies – But the Lottery-based System is Pulling Communities Apart'. *The Conversation*, 15 May 2023. Accessed 25 May 2023. https://theconversation.com/ethiopia-has-one -of-africas-most-ambitious-housing-policies-but-the-lottery-based-system-is-pulling -communities-apart-204816.

Martin, Michael T. and Gaston J.M. Kaboré, eds. 'On Decoloniality: African and Diasporic Cinema'. In *African Cinema: Manifesto and Practice for Cultural Decolonization*. Volume 3: *The Documentary Record—Declarations, Resolutions, Manifestos, Speeches*. Bloomington, IN: Indiana University Press, 2023.

Martin, Stewart. 'A New World Art? Documenting Documenta 11'. *Radical Philosophy* 122 (November/December 2003). Accessed 3 January 2022. https://www .radicalphilosophy.com/article/a-new-world-art.

Mbembe, Achille. 'The Idea of a Borderless World'. *Africa is a Country*, (opinion website) 11 November 2018. Accessed 23 May 2022. https://africasacountry.com/2018/11/ the-idea-of-a-borderless-world.

Mbembe, Achille. *Brutalisme*. Paris: La Découverte, 2020.

Mbembe, Achille. 'Coloniality of Infrastructure'. *e-flux*. October 2021. Accessed 23 May 2022. https://www.eflux.com/architecture/coloniality-infrastructure/410015/the -earthly-community/.

Mbembe, Achille. *La Communauté terrestre*. Paris: La Découverte, 2023.

Mbembe, Achille and Felwine Sarr, eds. *To Write the Africa World*. Translated by Drew Burk, London: Polity Books, 2022. Introduction, 'Thinking for a New Century'. (book excerpt), *Brittle Paper.com*, 16 February 2023. Accessed 8 August 2023. https:// brittlepaper.com/2023/02/excerpt-to-write-the-africa-world-edited-by-achille -mbembe-and-felwine-sarr-translated-by-drew-burk/.

Mbembe, Achille and Felwine Sarr, eds. *The Politics of Time: Imagining African Becomings*. Translated by Philip Gerard. London: Polity Books, 2023.

Meuser, Philipp and Adil Dalbai, eds. *Sub-Saharan Africa: An Architectural Guide*. Series, 6 vols (7 books). Berlin: DOM Publishers, 2021.

Mutata, Addamms. *Crisis Urbanism and Postcolonial African Cities in Postmillennial Cinema*. Oxon, New York: Routledge, 2022.

Petty, Sheila J. '"How an African Woman Can Be": African Women Filmmakers Construct Women'. *Discourse* 18, no. 3 (Spring 1996): 81.

Petty, Sheila J. 'The Archeology of Origin: Transnational Visions of Africa in a Borderless Cinema'. *African Studies Review* 42, no. 2 (September 1999): 73–86. https://doi.org/10 .2307/525365.

Petty, Sheila J. 'The Metropolitan Myth: Assimilation, Racism and Cultural Devaluation in "Soleil O" and "Pièces d'Identités"'. *L'Esprit Créateur* 41, no. 3 (2001): 163–171. http://www.jstor.org/stable/26288462.

Petty, Sheila J. '"Interstitial Spaces and Sites of Struggle": Displacement, Identity, and Belonging in Contemporary French Accented Cinema'. *Mashriq & Mahjar Journal of Middle East and North African Migration Studies* 9, no. 1 (2022): 121–143.

Pfaff, Françoise. 'African Cities as Cinematic Texts'. In *Focus on African Films*. Edited by Françoise Pfaff. Bloomington and Indianapolis: Indiana University Press, 2004, 89–106.

Rahbaran, Shadi and Manuel Herz. *Nairobi, Kenya: Migration Shaping the City*. ETH Studio Basel. Edited by Jacques Herzog and Pierre de Meuron. Zurich: Lars Müller Publishers, 2014.

Rodenbeck, Judith. 'Maison Tropicale: A Conversation with Manthia Diawara'. *October* no. 133 (Summer 2010): 106–132. Accessed 21 November 2023. https://doi.org/10.1162/OCTO_a_00005.

Sarr, Felwine. *Habiter le monde*. Paris: Cadastres, 2017.

Sarr, Felwine. *Afrotopia*. Translated by Drew S. Burk and Sarah Jones-Boardman. Minneapolis: University of Minnesota Press, 2020. https://doi.org/10.5749/j.ctv105bb1g.

Sarr, Felwine. *Afrotopia*. Paris: Philippe Rey, 2022.

Sherzer, Dina. *Cinema, Colonialism, PostColonialism, Perspectives from the French and Francophone Worlds*. Austin: University of Texas Press, 1996.

Siddiqi, Anooradha Iyer. 'Writing With: Togethering, Difference, and Feminist Architectural Histories of Migration'. *e-flux*. July 2018, Accessed 20 February 2022. https://www.e-flux.com/architecture/structuralinstability/208707/writing-with/.

Siddiqi, Anooradha Iyer. *Architecture of Migration: The Dadaab Refugee Camps*. Durham, NC: Duke University Press, 2024.

Simone, AbdouMaliq. *City Life from Jakarta to Dakar: Movement on the Crossroads*. New York; London: Routledge, 2010.

Stanek, Łukasz. *Architecture in Global Socialism: Eastern Europe, West Africa, and the Middle East in the Cold War*. Princeton, NJ: Princeton University Press, 2020.

Tayob, Huda. 'Reading Architecture through La Noire de…'. For the Multidisciplinary Research Project, *Centring Africa: Postcolonial Perspectives on Architecture*. Canadian Centre for Architecture. Accessed 3 January 2022. https://www.cca.qc.ca/en/articles/78256/reading-architecture-through-la-noirede?

The Filming of *Yeelen* by Souleymane Cissé, (Following the director on set), Accessed 6 November 2023. https://www.ina.fr/ina-eclaire-actu/video/i13175595/tournage-de-yeelen-de-souleymane-cisse.

Williams, James S. *Ethics and Aesthetics in Contemporary African Cinema*. London; New York: Bloomsbury Academic, 2019.

Winters, Christopher. 'Urban Morphogenesis in Francophone Black Africa'. *Geographical Review* 72, no. 2 (1982): 139–154.

Filmography

Amuli, Yuhi, director. *A Taste of Our Land*. Rwanda/Uganda, 2020 70 min.

Benhadj, Rachid, director. *Matares*. Algeria, 2019 90 min.

Cissé, Souleymane, director, *Yeelen, (La lumière)*. Mali, 1987 105 min.

Cissé, Soussaba, director. *Bogo Ja*. Mali, 2020 52 min.

Coulibaly Gillard, Simon, director. *Aya*. France/Belgium, 2021 91 min.

Diawara, Manthia, director, *Maison Tropicale*. Portugal, 2008 58 min.

Edkins, Teboho, director, *Days of Cannibalism: Of Pioneers, Cows and Capital*. Lesotho/France/South Africa/Netherlands, 2020 78 min.

Esiri, Arie and Chuko, directors. *Eyimofe* (*This is My Desire*). Nigeria, 2020 116 min.

Faye, Safi, director. *Kaddu Beykat* (*Lettre paysanne*). Senegal, 1975 90 min.

Ferhani, Hassen, director. *143 rue du désert* (*143 Desert Street*). Algeria/France/Qatar, 2019–2020 100 min.

Hondo, Med, director. *Soleil Ô* (*Oh Sun*). France/Mauritania, 1970 98 min.

Kaboré, Gaston, director. *Zan Boko* (*Homeland*). Burkina Faso, 1988 95 min. https://www.trigon-film.org/fr/movies/Zan_Boko.

Kahiu, Wanuri, director. *Pumzi*. Kenya, 2009 20 min.

Kahiu, Wanuri, director. *Rafiki*. Kenya, 2018 83 min. https://www.imdb.com/title/tt8286894/?ref_=nm_flmg_dr_4.

Loubière, Thomas, director. Co-writer Maud Rivière. *Le Camp suspendu*. France/Chad, 2020 70 min. https://vraivrai-films.fr/blog/le_camp_suspendu_fr.

Maïga, Aïssa, director. *Marcher sur l'eau* (*Above Water*). France, 2021 90 min. https://www.imdb.com/title/tt15001002/.

Mambéty, Djibril Diop, director. *Touki-Bouki* (*The Hyena's journey, Le Voyage de la hyène*). Senegal, 1973 88 min.

Mambéty, Djibril Diop, director. *Hyènes* (*Hyenas*). Senegal, 1992 113 min.

Mambéty, Djibril Diop, director. *La Petite Vendeuse de soleil* (*The Little Girl who sold the Sun*). Senegal/Switzerland, 1999 45 min.

Marescot, Luc, director. *Poumon Vert et Tapis Rouge* (*Green Forests and the Red Carpet*). France, 2021 95 min. https://www.imdb.com/title/tt13322906/.

Meddeb, Hind and Thim Naccache, directors. *Paris Stalingrad*. France, 2019 88 min.

Mirghani, Suzannah, director. *Al-Sit*. Sudan/Qatar, 2021 20 min.

Mora-Kpaï, Idrissou, director. *Arlit: Deuxième Paris*. Niger/France, 2004 98 min. https://newsreel.org/video/arlit-deuxieme-paris. https://video.alexanderstreet.com/watch/arlit-deuxieme-paris.

Nayar, Anjali, director. *Oil and Water*. Kenya/Canada, 2020 13 min.

Okoth Ochieng, Stephen, director. *Raindrops*. Nigeria, 2019 3 min.

Saguirou, Malam, director. *Solaire Made in Africa*. Niger, 2017 67 min.

Samassékou, Ousmane Zoromé, director. *The Last Shelter* (*Le dernier refuge*). France/Mali/South Africa, 2021 86 min.

Scarpelli, Mo, director. *Anbessa*. Ethiopia/Italy, 2019 86 min.

Schafer, Nicole, director. *Buddha in Africa*. South Africa, 2020 90 min.

Sembène, Ousmane, director. *Borom Sarret* (*the Wagoner, Le Charretier*). Senegal, 1963 20 min.

Sembène, Ousmane, director. *Ceddo* (*Outsiders*). Senegal, 1977 120 min.

(re-released, Three Revolutionary Films by Ousmane Sembène, *Emitaï* 1971, *Xala* 1975, *Ceddo* 1977. The Criterion Collection 2024). Accessed 30 June 2024. https://www.criterion.com/boxsets/7304-three-revolutionary-films-by-ousmane-sembene. https://www.youtube.com/watch?v=9ipcync79CI.

Serena, Marc, director. *The Writer from a Country Without Bookstores*. Spain, 2019 79 min.

Touré, Seidou Samba, director. *Massüba, le mal d'un people*. Burkina Faso, 2021 62 min.

Védrine, Laurent, director. *Restitutuer l'art Africain: les fantômes de la colonisation*. France, 2020 65 min.

Yotomane, Marlyse Awa, director. *Lucie*. Central Africain Republic, 2018 25 min.

INDEX

Printed in the USA
CPSIA information can be obtained
at www.ICGtesting.com
JSHW081208141124
73614JS00001B/5